Winning The Wealth Game

By Protecting Your Assets

Mark Robinson

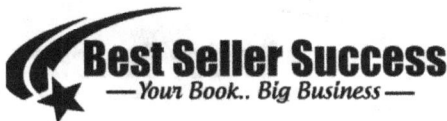

Best Seller Success
—Your Book.. Big Business—

All correspondence to the author
Acquire Wealth Solutions
PO Box 648
Moffat Beach
Qld 4551
Australia

Category: Investment: Finance: Wealth Creation & Preservation

Best Seller Success
— *Your Book.. Big Business* —

I would like to dedicate the book to our amazing team at the Acquire Group of Companies. I am extremely grateful for all the hard work you do. Your desire and passion are truly inspiring - thank you!

There are thousands of books out there that show you how to create wealth, but this is the only book you need to keep it. Work out what you are prepared to lose and insure yourself for the difference.

~ Mark Robinson

About the Author

Mark Robinson, founder and CEO of Acquire Wealth Solutions loves nothing more than helping Business Owners and Property Investors set up, grow and protect their wealth. His actions speak for themselves, creating seven successful companies in a four year period as well as a charity dedicated to a hand-up not a hand-out approach. His last company broke even in three months, profitable in six and hit a six figure income in nine months. His clients describe Mark as very professional and proactive with his advice.

Author, International Speaker, Investor and Entrepreneur Coach

Mark has written eight books and has been involved with over $251 million dollars worth of property transactions for his clients.

Mark has an ability to translate the complexities of the modern financial world into a simple easy-to-understand language. This allows his clients to grasp his recommendations with the understanding required to succeed. Mark uses a simple formula that looks at where you are today, where you want to be and then we work out which steps will be the best for you to get you there. Mark always works with the end in mind. What you are trying to achieve is foremost in his mind. Mark has the ability to help you take what you have learnt in seminars, webinars etc, and turn it into a viable and actionable financial plan.

This means we can look at all scenarios and not be stuck with traditional thinking. We will look at property, shares, managed funds, superannuation and businesses. You see most traditional Financial Planners will only look at managed funds because they just do not understand property or business. "Why planners overlook property and businesses is beyond me" Mark states.

Mark loves helping business owners increase their profits and exposure using the latest information and technology, such as Infusionsoft, Facebook, Twitter and LinkedIn.

ACQUIRE WEALTH SOLUTIONS

Personal

Mark lives on the beautiful Sunshine Coast with his wife Billie and two gorgeous girls, Jasmine-Rose and Rile-Jane, plus two dogs and a cat. He loves nothing more than spending time with his family either relaxing by the pool or down at the park or beach. He loves to travel and has spent time in Europe, Asia, USA, New Zealand and has been across most of Australia.

Education and Experience

Licensed Financial Planner. Diploma in Financial Services and Financial Planning. Diploma in Financial Services Mortgage Broking. Mark Robinson is an Authorized Representative, No 243170 of SMSF Partners Pty Ltd, and AFSL No 345905

Mark has authored and co-authored a number of books. The Wealth Game and Winning the Wealth Game book series. Titles include:

Winning the Wealth Game by Protecting Your Assets.

Winning the Wealth Game in Business.

Winning the Wealth Game by Creating Multiple Streams of Income. Winning the Wealth Game Trading Shares.

Winning the Wealth Game Using Property.

Winning the Wealth Game Online.

Winning the Wealth Game in Network Marketing.

Winning the Wealth Game for Women and many more.

Helping Business Owners and Property Investors to set up, grow and protect their Wealth.

The difference between ordinary & the extraordinary is that little extra.

~ **Unknown**

A note from the author...

I hope that the information in this book is useful to you and others who seek to protect their hard-earned money in these troubling times. Protecting wealth nowadays has become even more important than growing wealth. The emphasis now is keeping on to what you've worked your whole life to achieve, and that can be very tricky and perilous as well.

Make sure you make use of the Free Bonuses included in this book to ensure that you are protected at whatever stage you are on within the wealth cycle. 'Insure what you cannot afford to lose' is a favorite saying of mine and I hope by reading this book, it will help you determine what you have and what you are prepared to lose so that you can then insure yourself for the difference.

Sincerely,

Mark Robinson

Contents

Introduction

Forbes Magazine, in its annual list of the richest people in the world, reports that American billionaire Bill Gates is no longer the world's richest man. He's been out-ranked by Mexico's Carlos Slim Helu, whose various telecom holdings have a net worth of about $53.5 billion.

According to Forbes, much of the world's wealth came from Asia and Australia, whose 40 richest have a combined net worth of about $48.8 billion, up 45% from May 2009. Australia's richest solidified their haul mostly on the back of a healthy Australian dollar which gained 21% against the US greenback.

The bulk of Australia's wealth is in mines, which is worth about $8.5 billion. Andrew Forrest reigns supreme in this sector. Forrest reclaimed the top spot with his Fortescue Metals Group, which produces iron ore in Western Australia. Forrest's holding increased by 149%, helped partly by rising commodity prices and Chinese demand.

Forbes' list, however, also tracked down several Australian fortunes which took a dive during the global economic slump, including former billionaire Kerry Stokes who now ranks No. 22, and onetime billionaire Terry Peabody who dropped out of the list altogether.

What does it mean when billionaires' fortune shrinks and they lose money? It means that even the extremely rich are not immune to market and economic forces that could rob their wealth of its value. It also illustrates the fact that wealth protection should be as important as making it; that without a sound protection strategy, fortunes can shrink and vanish in a blink of an eye.

With the world economy plunging into uncertainty, people losing jobs and property being devalued, wealth has lost some of its power to intimidate. Wealthy people nowadays have the same problem as anyone else: how to protect their assets from death, divorce, serious illness, injury, and creditors.

You may think that wealth offers automatic protection against such attacks but it doesn't. Wealth can shrink, assets can be taken away if you are sued, file for bankruptcy, or subject to judgment proceedings.

Nowadays, asset protection is no longer the singular province of doctors, corporate executives and other litigation-prone professions. It now concerns everyone, because wealth can be subjected to litigation even in the most insignificant circumstances most people don't even consider until they occur. For instance, your dog knocks over an old guy hobbling on a cane on his way from getting the papers. The old guy breaks a hip and he sues you for damages. It doesn't matter that it was your dog that did the damage. Your dog is your responsibility and you're being sued because you didn't put him on a leash in the first place.

Understanding that wealth is vulnerable and that it needs protection is one way of shielding your assets not only from shrinking but being lost.

Social entrepreneur and wealth dynamics founder Roger Hamilton calls asset protection part of the 'low' of building wealth. He suggests that entrepreneurs need to do a 'wealth profile' of themselves, their partners and business associates so they'll have an idea of their strengths and weaknesses, the value they need to own, and how to secure leverage to maintain and protect their wealth.

Mr. Hamilton lists these eight wealth profiles as:

- The creator, who generates wealth from products (Bill Gates, Walt Disney)

- The star, who generates wealth from personal brand (Michael Jordan, Michael Jackson, Madonna)

- The supporter, who generates leadership (Jack Welch, Steve Case)

- The deal maker, who generates wealth from the deal (Donald Trump, Rupert Murdoch)

- The trader, who generates wealth from trades (George Soros, Kirk Kerkorian)

- The accumulator, who generates wealth from appreciation (Warren Buffet, Paul Allen)

- The Lord, who generates wealth from cash flow (John D. Rockefeller, John Paul Getty)

- The mechanic, who generates wealth from system (Sam Walton, Ray Kroc, Jeff Bezos)

Mr. Hamilton suggests that unless you know what type of profile you have as a wealth creator, you are likely to make mistakes in keeping and maintaining your wealth. It's going to be a hit and miss thing if you don't know your wealth profile. You will earn a lot of money but will probably not know how to keep it because your mind will be focused on something else. For example, you're an accumulator dreaming to be a star, or a mechanic itching to be a trader. If you try to be both, said Mr. Hamilton, you will fail.

This book therefore seeks to enlighten readers about wealth accumulation and protection. There's really no conflict between the two because each is part of the same cycle of wealth creation.

There may be hundreds of books that will show you how to create and protect wealth but you only need this one to keep it. Accidents do happen, and wealth can lose its value unless you know how to keep and protect it.

Measuring Your Risk

Prior to investing, you will need to measure your attitude to risks (what you are prepared to risk) then look to insure the difference.

Investing is the process of making your money work for you. It should not be viewed as a sacrifice. Investing is about helping your money keep up with your changing needs - it is not simply about building that retirement 'nest egg'.

As an investor, time is your best friend. Thus, it makes sense to get some professional help rather than simply waiting for the 'right time' before you start investing. But how you proceed depends on:

- Your particular financial situation, objective and needs;

- The investment strategies that you choose; and

- The amount of time you have.

Lastly, your attitude towards risk is one of the most important facets you could possess that could help boost your investment skills. The following list could help you identify what kind of risk-taker you are:

Low risk: If you're a very cautious investor who wants to protect the value of your investment over the short-term, this is your category. As a low-risk taker, you inherently feel more comfortable with cash and fixed-interest investments.

Low-to-medium risk: You're seeking a relatively low-risk investment over a medium length timeframe. Investors in this category not only want stability, but also some increment in the value of their investments.

Medium-to-high risk: If you feel most comfortable with a greater weighting towards investment types like Australian and international shares, this option may be for you. It has an investment timeframe of five years or more and has the potential for strong growth.

High risk: If you're willing to take a higher level of risk, in exchange for potentially greater earnings and want to invest over the long-term, then this investment category may be suitable for you. It's more beneficial for those with a long-term timeframe, and is not recommended for investors who require income from their investments or those who only have short investment timeframes.

Very high risk: In this category, you'll need to be prepared to take on higher risk in pursuit of potentially greater earnings.

Identify your age group

You should understand the advantages and limitations that may impact your investment strategy as a result of your age group. Select your age group from the following list:

Twenties

If you're still in your twenties, you may want to finish your education, party hard, travel, start a career, find a partner, buy your first home, etc. Your whole life is ahead of you, so putting money aside for the future may be a very low priority at this point.

But this is actually the best time to start investing simply because you have plenty of time ahead of you to recover from the inevitable market downturns and profit from the upturns. This is the time when higher-risk strategies could pay off. Your challenge is in finding the spare cash to invest.

Here are some options:

1. *Save your first home deposit.* Transfer a little cash each month into a high interest savings account or managed fund (depending on when you plan to buy, and the level of risk you're comfortable with).

2. *Take control of your investments.* Your superannuation monies from part-time jobs may be scattered all over. Even though you can't use the money now, superannuation is one of the largest investments you'll have, so roll it all into one place, and decide where and how to invest it.

3. *Start early with superannuation.* Returns compound over time, so if you've started your career, invest a little extra now and reap the benefits later. Ask your employer or financial planner about the tax benefits of salary sacrificing into your superannuation fund.

4. *Decide how much to invest.* Set realistic goals and a budget that lets you enjoy life, but put some money aside to save or invest. Pay yourself first by using a regular investment plan to drip-feed money from your transaction account into a managed fund or superannuation.

5. *If you're adventurous, consider borrowing to invest.* Gearing works by using borrowed money to invest. It has the potential to accelerate your wealth by magnifying investment gains, and can also magnify investment losses. Even if you start small, you could gradually transfer funds from a margin loan to a managed fund each month.

6. *Learn about investing and trading shares.* You may be able to use money you've already saved to invest directly in shares.

Thirties

This is the time when most people settle down, get married, start a family, return to work, change jobs, start their own business, get a new car or boat, take time out for a holiday, work overseas, or even pay off the mortgage.

Your income is probably increasing, but so are your expenses. If you didn't start investing in your twenties, you'll already be a few steps behind from those who did. Still, there are plenty of ways to get ahead and not substantially reduce the money available to you for day-to-day expenses.

You can catch up by doing the following:

1. *Repay your home loan faster.* If you have a variable rate property loan, you can pay more than you need to build a buffer against interest rate increases or for emergency cash. Once you feel your home loan is under control, a home gearing strategy could help you pay it off sooner. Gearing uses equity (the difference between the value of your property and how much you have left to pay on your mortgage) as security for a loan to invest in shares or managed funds. Income generated from your investments is then applied back into the home loan to help repay it faster. You should be aware that gearing can magnify investment gains but can also magnify losses in the event of economic downturn cycles.

2. *Protect your income and assets.* If you rely on your income to pay loans and bills, consider what would happen if you were to lose your earning capacity. Talk to your financial planner about how much life insurance or income protection you need, and how it could be tax effective.

3. *Pay less tax.* The amount of tax you pay increases as your income increases. Borrowing to invest (as discussed in # 1) is a great way to boost the size of your investment portfolio, and can also be tax effective because the loan interest may be tax deductible against investment earnings. If your spouse is not working, consider making contributions to your superannuation as you could get a tax rebate. If you're both working, an insurance bond can be a tax-effective way to save for other goals such as your children's education.

Forties

This is the period in life when you are inclined to focus on health and lifestyle, look to the future, wish you had more spare time, further your education, redundancy, self-employment, inheritance. Your children may be still at school or already leaving home. This is the time when you tend to realize that the time left to build up a decent nest egg is finite. Will your superannuation be enough by itself? The honest answer for many of us is no. What options are available that could help make sure of that by the time you retire?

You could:

1. *Increase your nest egg.* If you're earning more than you were in your thirties, and have repaid most, if not all of your home loan, you may be able to invest more in managed funds, shares or superannuation.

2. *Take control of your retirement.* Now is a good time to take a retirement reality check. Will you have enough to fund the lifestyle you want? A financial planner can tell you whether you're on the right track or not. He can advise you regarding options for your retirement needs as well as recommend strategies like salary sacrificing into superannuation to help close any gaps in your plans.

3. *Diversify outside of property.* If your biggest investment so far has been in property, it's probably increased in value. Now may be the time to consider how it could be put to work for you. Increase the size of your investment portfolio and diversify into other asset classes like shares by using your home equity*. The interest on the loan may be tax deductible against investment earnings. Remember, too, that gearing can also magnify investment losses in the event of an economic downturn.

4. *Invest lump sums wisely.* If you receive a lump sum payment (e.g. redundancy, inheritance, etc.) seek professional advice from your financial planner before deciding what to do with it.

---

*the difference between the value of your property and how much you have left to pay on your mortgage.

Fifties

This is the time in life when you are likely to experience 'empty nesting', children's university fees, wedding expenses, ageing relatives, job security concerns, health issues, redundancy, holiday home, overseas holiday, acquiring a small business, and so on.

There are still a number of options for you to consider at this stage of your life:

1. *Plan your retirement.* Once you retire, you usually can't contribute to superannuation, so act now to make the most of tax advantages that may still be available. For example, if you're thinking of downsizing your home when you retire, consider doing it sooner. You could invest the proceeds in superannuation and still enjoy the tax benefits. A financial planner will discuss transition strategies that could help maximize the tax effectiveness of your retirement plans.

2. *Increase the size of your portfolio.* If you've paid off your mortgage, consider how you could increase the size of your investment portfolio by using that extra cash. If you haven't diversified outside of real property by using a home gearing strategy, you may want to consider Option #3 under 'Forties'.

3. *Buy a small business or work part-time.* If the idea of retirement seems daunting, think about what type of retirement you'd like. For some, a small business, working part-time or attending further education may suit.

Retirement

It's worth remembering that your investment timeframe doesn't end when you retire. This is the time in life when you may face health issues, help the children get established, choose a sea-change, work part-time, take up a hobby, seek more education, take an extended holiday, lower your golf handicap, spoil your grandchildren, etc. Just because you've stopped working full-time doesn't mean that your money should. It's at this stage that most people adopt a more conservative approach to investing. There are still plenty of options, but choosing the right ones can be tough.

Here are a few options:

1. *Make your money last.* Despite retiring from the workforce, you may still have to plan for the next thirty or forty years. On one hand, you may have plenty of time to ride the ups and downs of the market. On the other hand, you want to protect your capital. You may consider a 'Retirement Investment Strategy' whereby you split your investment portfolio across low, medium and high growth assets depending on when you need the funds. You can invest in conservative asset classes for your immediate income needs and in potentially higher growth asset classes for your long term needs so that inflation doesn't erode the value of your investment.

2. *Maximize your income.* Senior Australians will be able to pay less income tax if they are eligible for the seniors offset, based on their age and income. It covers males aged 65 years or more and females aged 63 years or more

who are entitled to receive pensions and are Australian residents. The offsets also apply to veterans. The amount of income a senior Australian eligible for the seniors offset can earn before having to pay income tax will increase to $28,867 in 2008-09, up from $25,867 in 2007-08. For a senior couple, the tax-free threshold for their combined income will rise to $49,360, up from $43,360 (excluding offset).

The tax-free thresholds again rise in 2009-10 to $29,867 and $51,360 for a single senior and couple, respectively. Again, in 2010-11, the levels rise respectively to $30,685 and $53,360. That's a sizable jump in money which will now be exempt from tax if seniors qualify for the SATO.

The Federal Government has also changed Medicare Levy thresholds for SATO recipients to ensure they do not pay the Medicare Levy until their taxable income passes these new tax-free thresholds.

The Federal Government has extended the Low Income Tax Offset (LITO) which increases to $1200 from $750 from 2008-09, reducing once taxable income reaches $30,000 and cutting out entirely at $60,000. It will further increase to $1,350 from July 2009 and $1,500 from July 2010.

For retirees eligible for the low-income threshold, they can now receive tax-free income of $14,000 if single (up from $11,000) or $28,000 for a couple (up from $22,000).

For retirees aged less than 60 years who are receiving a pension income from their superannuation, they will now be able to earn a taxable income of $44,210 per annum if they are single and $88,420 as a couple before paying income tax.

These figures assume eligibility or the Senior Australian Tax Offset and is dependent on individual circumstances and age, conditions apply and a Medicare Levy is payable. Ask your Financial Planner how you could maximize your income in retirement, and how you might be able to obtain a government pension. This may involve rolling your superannuation into an allocated pension or complying pension.

3. *Check your will and estate plan.* Circumstances change and estate planning can be a complex area. To help you to allocate the right thing to the right person at the right time, you should meet with a legal expert to discuss your will and estate plan.

When I hear somebody sigh 'life is hard,' I am always tempted to ask 'compared to what'?

~ Sydney Harris

Whenever you find yourself on the side of the majority, it is time to pause and reflect.

~ Mark Twain

STEP - 1

Entities
For
Wealth
Protection

Actions speak louder than words.

- Proverb

Before we go into the details of wealth protection, it might be better if we first define what it means.

Wealth protection is a strategy in which assets or wealth is protected against risk. What are the types of these assets? They can be in the form of a family home, a car, a business, a share portfolio, an investment real estate, valuable artworks, and many more. Who are the people who need this protection strategy?

There are four major groups:

- The very wealthy

- Those in the public eye who are prime targets for litigators and regulators

- People who own a business and/or engaged in a professional occupation

- People who suspect they might be a future target of legal, financial or even medical difficulty

Why do you need a wealth protection strategy? Because it acts as a shield against any crippling government penalties you may incur in the course of business, claims by an ex-wife or de factor partner, claims by disgruntled business associates/ employees, and claims arising from an incident which caused a person to suffer a serious illness.

Here's one way of looking at asset protection: You're in a bitter litigation fight with an ex-partner who's suing you for half of the business you put up together. This ex-partner, however, might give pause if s/he sees the barriers you have surrounding your assets to protect it.

The asset protection serves as an obstacle your ex-partner must jump over before s/he can get his/her hands on your business. They see this obstacle and may be encouraged to settle favorably instead of getting involved in a long and drawn-out litigation process.

What you could lose

Picture this: if you lose in a successful legal claim, liability action or bankruptcy case creditors will get their hands on your assets. The banks will have a field day disposing of your income, including your superannuation pension if any. Even if your claim is successful, it can be costly and a no win situation for you and your assets.

Who's at risk?

Everybody from directors, executives and small business owners are open to legal action from disgruntled employees, competitors, suppliers, debtors and the ATO under the Trade Practices Act, Corporation Act and income tax acts.

Professionals and tradespeople alike can face multi-million dollar claims. Sole traders are personally liable for the debts of their businesses, and must meet any liability or professional negligence claims made against the business. Even as a partner in a business, you are individually responsible for all claims made against the business.

Property owners, motorists and people who employ domestic staff, such as cleaners and gardeners, are now frequently subject to Workers Compensation, liability and negligence actions following accidents.

Ongoing risks

Another thing, your legal liability does not end when you sell your business/property even when you retire. They can be put at risk by claims arising from actions or events that happened many years ago.

Protecting your assets

There are many ways to protect an asset or wealth but like a portfolio, they should be diversified and not dependent on one method alone. Here are some ways to consider to protect your assets:

Transfer your assets to your spouse

This is not advice and should not be relied upon but in general the most practical way to protect your wealth is to transfer some of your assets to the name of your non-exposed spouse. In most cases, this generally means unencumbered assets like the family home. If the wife's name does not appear in any leases, and she has not signed any personal guarantees for trade debts, then the house is safe if the husband goes bankrupt.

A recent amendment to Australia's Bankruptcy Law, however, may put a damper on the effectiveness of this practice. Under the amendment, if the family home is in the wife's name and the husband goes bankrupt, the family home is still made vulnerable to a creditor attack unless the wife can prove she is meeting mortgage payments on the home from her own separate income.

Another thing to consider is what happens to the property if the spouse dies. In most cases, the asset automatically reverts back to the spouse's name and the heirs, barring some exemptions, may have to pay heavy stamp duty for its transfer.

Trusts

Not many people can differentiate between a Trust and a Will. The main difference between the two is the manner in which your property is being disposed of after your death. In a Will, property goes on probate (court system) to determine its legalities and the properties being distributed. The property may also become vulnerable to taxes and legal fees.

In a Trust, the property is transferred to a Trustee, whether an individual or corporation, while you are still alive and will continue after your death. Under a Trust, the property will avoid probate and may be shielded against heavy taxes, creditors, and divorce claims when you die. It also means you no longer own this property but it is owned by the trustees of the trust. You can, however, still have access to it in your lifetime and even instruct your Trustees who to leave it to after you die.

The trustee is the actual legal owner of the trust property since he is tasked to carry out its wishes. Trustees can also benefit from the trust. Trusts are generally cheaper to set up than most alternative options and no more costly to administer.

Trusts are advantageous since they can offer limited liability and income splitting possibilities for the beneficiaries and unit holders. Trusts have an 80-year life span, and all income must be distributed each year to avoid high tax rates.

Beneficiaries in a trust are generally classed into three types:

- Specified beneficiaries whom the trust was specially created, e.g., parents and children

- General class of beneficiary, which includes close relatives of the primary beneficiaries

- Tertiary class of beneficiary includes other trust or companies in which the beneficiary has an interest

There are eight types of trusts. Here we will focus on the most common.

1. Discretionary Trust

Commonly referred to as a family trust, this trust is often the preferred structure in asset protection strategies because it is the trustee who must be sued and not the individual beneficiaries or other associated persons. Where the trustee is a corporate entity then the 'owners' of the trust are usually fully protected from creditor claims against the trust by the corporate veil. A corporate trustee can therefore provide better asset protection to the individuals establishing the trust than would be afforded if they were to be trustee's in their own right. The distribution of income also provides a distinct tax advantage since it usually allows income to be distributed among the lower tax earners and even children, subject to the same limitation.

The discretionary trust, however, is generally not appropriate when trading or rental losses are expected. This is because they are quarantined within the trust and not available to be distributed to beneficiaries. Because of this, the trust may not be suitable for investors who apply negative gearing, unless income is also collected from other sources within the trust.

Success seems to be connected with action.
Successful people keep moving. They make
mistakes but don't quit.

~ Conrad Hilton

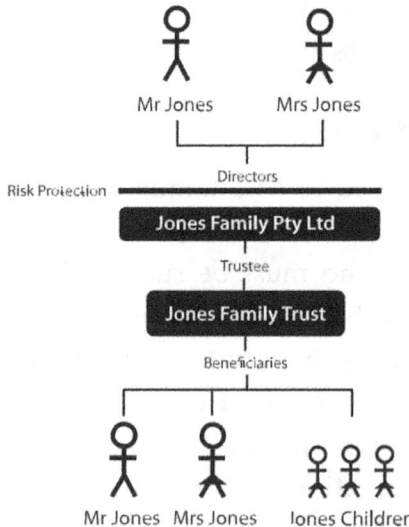

Mr. and Mrs. Jones and their children receive income from the Family Trust as determined by the trustee. That entitlement can change each year at the discretion of the Trustee, meaning the taxation outcome can be optimized as circumstances change over time.

2. Unit Trust

Unit trust involves beneficiaries (called unit holders) owning certain shares (called units) in a trust. Under a unit trust, unit holders are entitled to income and capital distributions from the unit trust on the number of units they own in the trust. Trustees can also generally own units in the unit trust.

Unit trusts work because people outside your family can own units, borrow money and run the business anytime. The trust, however, is not flexible especially in the distribution of income, which is pre-determined by the entitlements of unit holders. This can be modified but will often trigger capital gains tax* issues.

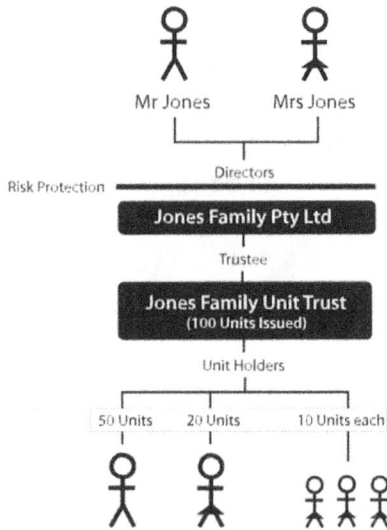

*Capital gains tax (CGT) is the tax you pay on any capital gain you include on your annual income tax return.

3. Hybrid Trust

Hybrid trusts combine the elements of both united discretionary trusts. In a hybrid trust, the trustee pays a certain amount to beneficiaries which are fixed by the settlor. The trustee is allowed to make both income and capital distributions to beneficiaries in ratio to the number of units they own. Beneficiaries can then claim tax deductions for items like interest on borrowing, which allows this type of structure to be used in negative gearing situations.

Generally, hybrid trusts are good for asset protection, 50% capital gains tax relief, and estate planning benefits. They become disadvantageous, however, if they're not correctly established or run, since they inevitably become unprotected and tax-challenged by the Tax Office.

4. Asset protection trusts

It's not unheard of for wealthy individuals to transfer a portion of their assets into an offshore trust to protect them from creditors and shield the assets for their children.

Besides the Cook Islands and Nevis, popular asset protection trusts are found in several American states including Alaska, Delaware, Rhode Island, Nevada and South Dakota. You may not need to be a resident of these states to set up an asset protection trust. However, you need to study the state laws carefully since one of the requirements of this type of trust is that it must be irrevocable and the laws can change.

Other requirements for an asset protection trust may include:

- The trust must have an independent trustee, whether an individual, bank or trust company licensed in that state.

- It allows distributions at the trustee's discretion.

- It should include a spendthrift clause.

- Some or all of the trust's assets should be located in the trust's state.

- All documents and administration must be in the state.

These trusts are the most expensive to establish and maintain and are generally only appropriate in specific situations.

Less Complex Ways to Protect Assets

The following are other inexpensive ways to protect your assets:

- Try funneling more money into your employer-sponsored retirement plan. The tax benefits could be endless.

- Hold member entitlements in SMSF's* in a reserve account rather than in the members' entitlement account.

- Consider licensing high value assets so they are not directly owned by the entity exposed to the risk.

- Invest in insurance that gives shelter against personal-injury claims.

- Take advantage of laws regarding homesteads, annuities and life insurance.

- Avoid mixing business assets with personal assets. That way, if your company runs into a problem, your personal assets may be shielded from risks.

* Self Managed Super Fund

Do you have an accountant who *ACTIVELY* works with you to achieve YOUR wealth and lifestyle goals?

DOES YOUR ACCOUNTANT ?	yes	no
1. **Know (or care!!) what YOU** want to achieve out of business and life?		
2. Help you identify **your vision** for your future, **your goals** and the **steps to get you there?**		
3. **Work with YOU** to develop a strategy to achieve those business and personal goals?		
4. Have a team of experts in the field of wealth creation at their fingertips. We mean fully qualified and licensed **EXPERTS**, not just pretenders.		
5. Have a team that is dedicated to and exclusively focused on **YOU** and **YOUR** success.		
6. Offer assistance on **how to convert more leads into sales?**		
7. Provide feedback and **new ideas** on your **marketing and advertising** to generate a much better return for your dollar?		
8. Establish KPI's and the tools to measure, manage and improve your performance.		
9. Proactively **monitor your progress** so you can adjust quickly and build profits and wealth?		
10. Charge you a yearly, **all inclusive fee paid monthly**, rather than an hourly rate fee which see **YOU** **paying to fix their mistakes?**		
11. Provide free unlimited phone and email support?		
12. Work to constantly **increase your financial wealth**?		
13. **Provide $000's worth of FREE stuff?**		
14. Provide fully qualified and licensed financial advice?		
15. Have a laugh with **YOU** and enjoy your journey?		

HOW DID YOU GO?

I know it's not easy to find a decent accountant believe me. Remind me to share our story about accountants when we catch up. We do however in our team have access to the best accountants I have found. They all have different skill sets, from Self managed super funds, small business through to international tax laws. Give us a call and see which one will suit your needs.

STEP - 2

Financial Structure

Two roads diverged in the woods, and I took the one less travelled by, and that has made all the difference.

~ Robert Frost

Debt is part of the capital structure of any business. It's as important as any business strategy, a product idea or marketing scheme. In terms of financial structure, debt is just another investment and a lender just another investor.

It's not about consumer debt where you buy things you can't pay for right now. You borrow because you want to amplify the returns on equity, the ownership part of your capital structure.

In a nutshell, lenders (debt investors) help fund your business in exchange for a share in your revenues. Unlike equity investors who can participate in profits and gain in the business' value, lenders' return is limited only to the interests. However, they have first claim on your company's assets when the business topples over and goes bust. It's the nature of the beast and you have to be aware of the risks.

Payments on debt are often on top of the list of your obligations. Even if no money is coming in, you still have to pay the loan. In extreme cases, loan holders have the right to 'call' a loan – that is, demand full payment – when you violate the agreement of the debt (as in late payment, etc.).

Because of its strategic nature, if you don't understand what it's about and you get it wrong, you go bust.

Debt has a Janus-faced nature: great when the going is good but worse than your worst nightmare when the going is bad.

Types of loans

There are five main types of loans used to create wealth in Australia through property. These are standard variable, basic, fixed rate loan, line of credit and commercial loan.

Standard Variable loan

The standard variable rate loan in Australia is the benchmark loan rate for new loans lent here in Australia. It has a flexible rate which changes with the economic conditions of that particular time. The rate goes up and down with the market. It also allows flexibility such as redraw, extra payments can be made, lower discharge and exit fees.

Usually this rate is used for the basis of all professional packs in Australia. Major banks offer the professional pack which give discount rates off the standard variable rate and usually includes an annual fee and comes with features such as offset accounts, free credit cards, free transaction accounts and usually no account keeping fees for a loan.

The true benefit here is the flexibility of this type of loan. When you are an investor you want flexibility in your lending arrangements. For example, if you were to sell a property and you had a hundred thousand profit left over you would usually like that money to reduce the balance of another loan and reduce your interest costs. Also you might want to repay your owner occupied loan which is non-taxable debt.

Basic loan

The basic loan is very similar to the standard variable loan; however, it is a discounted loan and has no frills. It does have the main benefits of being variable and redraw is usually a feature. The loan is usually one basic loan with no splits. The interest can be either principal and interest or interest only. I will go into that further in this chapter.

This loan is great for a purchase of an investment property we need to set and forget. Usually there are no fees apart from an upfront or an application fee when applying for this loan. They do not usually come with offset accounts, credit cards transaction accounts etc; as the name implies it is a basic loan. However I do use loans quite a lot for investor clients purchasing new investment properties.

Fixed rate vs. standard variable loan

Interest rates in a fixed-rate mortgage loan never change during the 'fixed period' of the loan, regardless of what happens to the economy. Standard variable rates mortgages, on the other hand, have interest rates that adjust periodically during the life of the loan.

Pros & Cons of Fixed Mortgage Loans

The primary benefit of a fixed-rate loan is certainty. You know what your interest rates will be, even if the economy spins out of control. The downside is that you'll generally pay a premium for this predictability in the form of higher interest rates that may or may not be caught up by standard variable rates.

Mortgage lenders take on certain amount of risks in a fixed-rate loan. If the prime interest rate goes up during the life of your loan, the lender pays the difference not you, which is why in the beginning he charges a much higher interest rate than with a standard variable rates mortgage. Of course, the lender will factor their expectation of future interest rate movements and the actual rates may go up or down in a different manner. There are times when standard variable rates are higher than those of a fixed rate but this is not as common.

Pros & Cons of Standard variable rates Mortgage Loan

The interest rate in a standard variable rates loan is lower than a traditional fixed-rate mortgage because the fixed rates include an additional risk premium noted above. It can, however, be unpredictable since you'll never know what interest rate it will adjust to after the initial rate is established.

Interest rates could start off lower but may go higher during the life of the loan. Thus, your monthly payments can rise and fall with interest rates movements. Great if they fall, but definitely bad if they rise. This unpredictability can be rather nerve-wracking so standard variable rates loans may seem like a gamble.

Whether you take a fixed or floating loan will largely depend on how you view future interest rate movements and how important certainty of repayments is to your personal circumstances.

Line of Credit (LOC)

Borrowers can set up financing options by using a Line of Credit, before they find another property to buy. Since they already own the property the loan is based upon equity available in their existing property to draw down this loan.

This account is extremely important for an investor moving forward as it becomes a buffer account, or a surplus account, or an equity bucket. People call this by different names depending on who you talk to.

Line of credit loans are flexible and offer a range of features to borrowers. They require interest payments on outstanding balances to be made each month. They also need security or collateral to establish the line of credit. Line of credit loans allow payments in and withdrawals out according to the borrower's needs within a set maximum credit limit.

LOCs also provide access to the equity that has built up in an existing property similar to a credit card. You can access the line of credit when you need it and interest is charged on the outstanding balance.

Also on a true line of credit loan you have the ability to capitalise interest. This means that the interest that is due every month on this loan can capitalise in the loan account. For example you have $200,000 as a line of credit and you've drawn down.

$100,000 for use. The interest on that loan for one month may be $700. That money can increase the loan amount owing. Rather than making a regular payment, your loan balance would increase to $100,700. However, you may make a payment into your line of credit of $2000 to cover the interest for last month and this month and reduce your balance owing. This is really taking control of your cash and maximising its potential.

Advantages of line of credit loans

Line of credit loans have several advantages:

- You have the option to use the money when you need it and pay it back when you are able to.

- Since line of credit loans act like a transaction account, it can be used to purchase items besides real estate.

- LOCs offer greater flexibility as they allow you to manage the time you have to repay the loan and the amount of your payments. You can pay in amounts and draw funds as needed, which can reduce interest rate charges to a minimum.

- Since these loans are secured by a home, credit limits are higher while interest rates are lower than unsecured overdraft and personal loans.

  Whether buying another property or paying for a home renovation, debt line of credit loans offer an answer to a particular need.

- Most of the time, these loans are also attached to a professional pack, therefore reducing your fees and costs, otherwise there would generally be a monthly charge.

Disadvantages of line of credit loans

The downside of line of credit loans are the following:

- They have a higher interest rate than a traditional mortgage.

- The interest rate charged is slightly higher than a standard variable basic loan.

- Some level of discipline is need so the borrowed funds are not applied to consumer purchases, therefore creating non-tax deductible debt.

Commercial loans

The reason most investors get a commercial loan is for business use and the purchase of a commercial property. These loans are specifically designed for that purpose. Usually the loan interest repayments are about 1% to 2% higher than a residential mortgage-based loan. The bank's criteria on this type of loan are more stringent and they usually ask for cash or equity for the purchase. For example, if you were to buy a commercial factory warehouse they may only lend 70% of the purchase price of the property, whereas under a residential loan they may lend you up to 95% of the value of the property.

Commercial loans have similar features to a residential loan: they either come in variable or fixed rates, however usually a line of credit is not available.

Features of investment loans:

1. Interest Only Loan

Interest only loans are great for real estate investment especially if the property you intend to purchase has scope for significant capital growth. You only need to worry about paying the interest as part of your monthly payment during the interest only period but will not be required to service the principal balance until the end of the interest only period. At the end of the interest only period, you will either pay off the entire loan amount in one payment or the loan will revert to a principal and interest loan.

Interest only loans offer flexibility on a monthly basis. If you do not have the extra money, you simply make the minimum interest payment and move on. Depending on the loan terms, you may be able to service the principal balance by paying extra when you have surplus funds.

2. Converting a Principle & Interest Loan to Interest Only

Sometimes converting a loan from principal and interest repayments to an interest only repayment can free up monthly cash flow for you.

This can allow you to purchase an investment property if there was a shortfall on a property. Let me explain. Say you had a $400,000 mortgage where you are making principle and interest repayments. Let's say for example that you had a 7% interest rate, the monthly repayment for the loan would be $2659p/m. Now if we converted that to interest only repayments, the repayments would be $2333p/m.

This is a difference of $326p/m approximately. I then look to see how you could better utilise the surplus money. As you can see, very early on in the loan you're only making minimal principal repayments.

What might be better is that if you were to purchase an investment property and it was running at a loss of $75 per week then your shortfall could be covered because your other loan has been turned into an interest only loan. Now the reason we would do this, is that the investment property is likely to increase in value faster than you could actually pay principal debt off the other loan. For example, property prices in Australia usually double every 7 to 10 years as history has shown. If you're able to purchase a $400,000 property and it was costing you $75 dollars a week to hold that property in 10 years' time that property would be worth about $800,000.

If you were to sell the property and pay the $400,000 loan back to the bank, technically in basic math you would have another $400,000 to pay off the existing mortgage. Is this an easier way to repay a $400,000 mortgage over 10 years? I think so.

3. Fixed Payment Loan

Fixed payment loans allow you to pay the same payment every month for the life of the loan. It offers a lot of consistency, plus you are also servicing the principal balance of the loan. With this type of loan, you just make your monthly payments every month until the debt is retired at the end of the term.

This is a good loan strategy if you want to pay off the loan instead of refinancing it or selling it in the near future.

4. Private Investor

As its name implies, a private investor is a person who has lots of extra money to lend. If you find one, a private investor might be willing to work with you on purchasing an investment property. Private investors may be flexible and easy to work with compared to a bank. This makes a private loan a very enticing option to consider.

A private investor usually charges a lot more interest and sometimes wants to be equity or stakeholder in the actual proposed property purchase or development. Always check and read the fine print before enticing a private investor in on the property purchase.

Property Investment - the Pros & Cons

Property may be a good investment reason to take out a loan, but like other propositions, there are also pros and cons to it:

Pros:

- *Tax benefits* on repairs and maintenance, rates and taxes, insurance, agent's fees, travel to and from the property, depreciation.

- *Negative gearing* – when the costs of keeping the investment property exceed the income produced by it, significant tax benefits can be achieved when applied appropriately.

- *Long-term investment* – good idea for beefing up a retirement fund as rental housing is one sector that rarely decreases in value.

- *Positive asset base* – allows you to show potential lenders that you have the ability to maintain a loan without defaulting. Also, you can use the increase in the property value as further collateral when taking out another loan.

- *Safety aspect* – rental incomes from housing especially in metropolitan areas provide an annual gross yield of between 4.5% and 5.5%.

- *High leverage possibilities* – investment properties can be purchased at 90% to 95% LVR (loan to valuation ratio), which is calculated by taking the amount of the loan and dividing it by the value of the property as determined by the lender. This high leverage capacity results in a high investment return relative to your cash investment since up to 95% of the purchase price is provided by the mortgagee.

Cons:

- *Liquidity* – it can take months to sell the property if things go bad unless you're willing to accept a lower sale price.

- *Vacancies* – you will need to cover mortgage payments out of your own pocket if the property remains untenanted.

- *Bad tenants* – problem tenants are every investment property owner's worst nightmare. They can damage your property, refuse to pay rent, refuse to leave, or all of the above.

- *Ongoing costs* – in addition to other standard costs, ongoing maintenance costs can be expensive.

- *Putting all your eggs in one basket* – if you have all your money tied up in property and the market crashes you can stand to lose significantly.

- *Capital gains tax* – imposed by the government on the appreciation of investments and payable on disposal. These can be mitigated with appropriate structures in place and relevant professional advice.

Lending in today's environment

The economic crisis remains fresh and various bailout solutions are still untested, so it is difficult to predict what's going to happen next in the lending market. As things stand now, even if you have had a good relationship with your local lender, you are likely to find it harder to get more money on the terms you've enjoyed in the past.

For borrowers, it's critical to re-establish past relationships and perhaps cultivate new ones with more than one lender.

Lenders are more likely to grant a loan to companies with solid balance sheets than companies with weaker balance sheets. Also, companies with good track records in both good and bad markets will likely carry more weight with lenders.

Companies may be able to get loans but they may find the terms have changed. Interest rates are higher than they were previously and the type of covenants are harder to meet than they may have been in the past.

According to a recent report by the International Monetary Fund (IMF), the global financial sector faces a write-down of $4.1 trillion from the toxic assets that have crashed in value since the start of the credit crunch. The Fund said potential losses in the US alone will likely reach $2.7 trillion. Europe and Japan between them account for $1.3 trillion of the write-downs, with UK banks facing losses of up to $316 billion.

In Australia, the $1.2 billion write off made by the National Australia Bank (NAB) on its conduit US loans continue to reverberate in the lending industry. NAB had a number of big clients who wanted to invest in the US housing loans. When the property market crashed, the bank had to write off 90% of it's loans.

The effect on lenders was to tighten policies. They now insist, more than ever, that borrowers have a wealth of reliable information and credible sources to provide lenders. Any attempts to massage the numbers are most likely to be detected in today's environment and will result in the loan being turned down, and the borrower losing their credibility.

What the bank wants to see

In today's lending, banks are more likely to demand more than your overall capital net worth before lending you money. Part of their credit investigation is to see in your loan proposal the three important C's, which can be summarised as:

1. Character

Includes integrity, trustworthiness, credit score, and how the borrower has handled other financial obligations.

2. Capacity

Whether the borrower is operating within their abilities and not attempting to accomplish something beyond their limitations or means. This includes their position in the market, experience in the industry, track record in business, cash flow projections, and earning potentials.

3. Collateral

Refers to the borrower's ability to guarantee the loan with tangible assets as a secondary source of repayment i.e. property equity or cash as a source of repayment if you were to default on the loan.

Also important are, the nature of the business, current demand for products and services, inflation rates, interest rates, local and global economic conditions, labor conditions, current business trends and current losses that the lender suffers due to credit issues.

BONUS CHAPTER

The
7 Rules
of Equity

Here I'm going to give you the first two rules of my latest e-book *'The 7 Rules of Equity'.* For the other five chapters, please go to **www.acquirewealthsolutions.com.au**

The 7 rules of equity?

I hope you find the following content informative and use these seven rules for future purchases to build your portfolio.

Rule 1. Taking control of your equity

First of all, let me explain what equity is. Equity is the difference between the amount your properties are worth (e.g., $500,000) and the loan that you may have on a property (e.g., $300,000.) This would be viewed as equity of $200,000 in that property. Now, the bank that has your first registered mortgage over the property thinks that this is a fantastic position to be in as it's returning the bank $200,000 worth of asset protection on your property if you were to default on your loan and couldn't repay - so there would be plenty of buffer for the bank to potentially sell your property and recoup the $300,000 and any expenses, including all legal costs.

This puts the bank in a very powerful position - and who's really in control of your equity, you or the bank?

Now, if you are talking to a broker, finance specialist or your local bank manager, they may talk about LVR. LVR is Loan to Value Ratio (LVR). On the above scenario, the LVR on this property would be 60%. So potentially, there is 40% equity available in your property. Now, the banks and all other lending institutions will always want a percentage of equity that is needed for the purchase of a property - this covers the risk to the lender, in lending finance to you. This could be as low as a 5% margin in the property.

Loan Structure

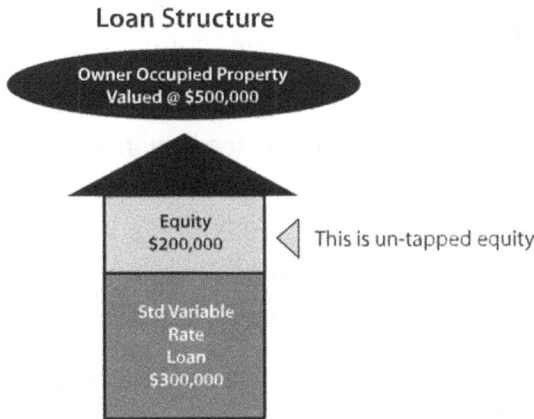

Owner Occupied Property
Valued @ $500,000

Equity
$200,000

This is un-tapped equity

Std Variable
Rate
Loan
$300,000

Showing you the equity available in your property.

In other words, you need to put in a 5% deposit towards the property purchase, but most likely, it's going to be more than 5% and more likely 20%.

There is usually Mortgage Insurance you may have to pay if you decide that your lending will be greater than 80% LVR. Lenders mortgage insurance is also referred to as LMI in the industry. Sometimes it is a good thing to pay LMI as it allows you to utilise the equity in your property to purchase more property. I will expand on this later in some of my other rules.

In most instances, when people come and see me for the first time, the bank will be in control of their equity, not the person who is actually paying the mortgage on the property.

So the first thing I show clients is how easy it is to actually tap into the equity in their property and use that to build their wealth portfolio - whether it's in property, shares, managed funds or other investments.

So the first rule is to take control of your equity and not to leave the bank in control of your equity. Completing this first step enables you to enter the wealth creation strategy!

Now do your calculation and see how much equity you have available. You may have $100,000 available, you may have $50,000 or you may have $10,000. It's all equity and in the end, it can be all turned into more investment purchases and finally turned into profits or cash - but I'll talk about that later.

Everyone remembers the TV advertisement 'equity mate'... that special the bank was always promoting - the one where you go out and buy your new car, jet-ski or holiday. This is exactly what you do not want to be spending your equity on. These items are not appreciating in value, but rather depreciating in value and will be worth far less in the future than when you originally purchased them. You should be looking to tap into equity to use it to purchase income producing assets or assets that are going to grow and help you build more equity.

Rule 2. Tapping into the equity

You must first tap into your equity to put yourself back in control - not the banks. So you ask, "How do I go about tapping into the equity in my property?"

First of all, you need to talk to an experienced broker who understands your goals and your strategy. You can talk to your banker, but they're only going to be interested in making profits for the bank. All of the finance specialists at *Acquire Wealth Solutions* consider your situation and can help you (not the bank) make profits. We can show you how to do this.

We would first look at how much your properties are worth and then see how much debt you have against those properties. We also need to assess your serviceability to see that you can actually pull the equity out of your property, as this is very important. Once we have assessed your serviceability to be able to service the extra amount of money that you could take from your property, we'll go through and submit an application to a lender. That equity may be with your current bank or it may be with a new bank, as a new lender may have a higher serviceability level or a better product to suit your needs. This process usually takes about 4 to 5 weeks.

For example, in the above scenario we've got a property worth $500,000 and current debt with the lender at $300,000. We may take you to an 80% LVR which would increase your lending to $400,000 and give you $100,000 of equity to be used to move forward to purchase or help you use deposits for future property purchases.

What has this just done for you? This has enabled you to have access to a hundred thousand dollars that you can use for deposits for investment properties or wealth creation strategy techniques. This has put you back in control of your equity and the bank now only has control of 20%, where you have control of the other 80%. Yes, you may call this a loan, and that you owe the bank $400,000 - however if we're building your portfolio then we now have access to $ 100,000 which is then a tax deduction as long as we're using it for investment products such as property, shares, managed funds or other investment opportunities that you may come across. This is illustrated in the diagram opposite.

As you can see, this is a crucial step in taking control of your equity and tapping into the equity that you have in your existing property. In some cases, we may recommend that you actually take your lending up to 90% LVR. This puts you in control of your equity so the bank is only in control of 10%. This gives you stronger buying power to purchase more properties on the other end. For instance, if we had a $500,000 property and we're going to get a 90% loan, we would then have a new total lending of $450,000 made up of $300,000 existing debt (owner occupier debt) and $150,000 - the new equity loan.

Loan Structure

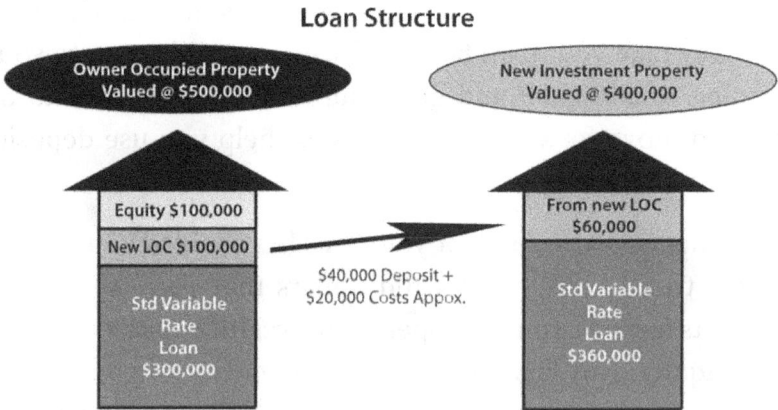

Showing you how to tap into your equity to purchase another property.

This gives us the possibility of perhaps buying two properties instead of one. This will help you build a property portfolio a lot faster.

So take action now and talk to one of our Acquire Wealth Solutions finance specialists to see how much untapped equity you have available to start your property portfolio!

STEP - 3

Risk Management

Feel the fear and do it anyway.

~ Susan Jeffers

Risk is defined as an event that has a probability of happening, and which could have a positive or negative impact on your business. A risk may have one or two causes, and if it happens, will have one or more impacts.

In business, for example, the identification of risk usually starts before you initiate a project. Risks accumulate as the project matures through its cycle. When you identify a risk, first ascertain its probability of occurring, the degree to which it will affect your business schedule, cost, and quality and then prioritise. The probability of occurrence and the degree of its impact (high, medium, low) will become the basis for assigning the risk priority.

Identifying a risk involves one important step: documenting the risk so you can mitigate and then make a contingency plan. Mitigation actions are often costly and can even exceed the cost of assuming the risk or incurring the consequences. Thus, it is important to evaluate the probability and impact of the risk against the mitigation strategy cost before you decide to implement the contingency plan. Contingency plans are pre-emptive actions intended to reduce the impact or remove the risk. When implemented after the risk occurs, it can only lessen, not cushion the impact of the risk.

How to manage risk

There are four ways you can manage risk. You can:

- *Accept it.* Simply accept that this is a risk. But in accepting it, you are also saying that you are not going to take any actions but will take responsibility for the cost, schedule, scope, and quality impacts if the risk happens again.

- *Transfer it.* You can shift the impact of a risk to a third party (like a sub-contractor). It does not eliminate risk but simply shifts responsibility. Another way to transfer the risk is through insurance.

- *Reduce it.* You can take steps to reduce the probability or impact of a risk by taking early action like close monitoring, more testing, etc.

- *Eliminate it.* You can also eliminate risk by changing the way you produce your product.

Risk management strategy

Risk management is not a one-off exercise since it involves continuous monitoring and reviewing of your risk management approach. Constant monitoring ensures that you have correctly identified and assessed the risk and are putting controls in place to lessen its impact.

All of this can be formalised in a risk management strategy, which clearly sets out your business' appetite for risk and its approach to risk management. Part of risk management is also assigning responsibility to chosen employees and getting support and commitment at the board level.

Following a good risk management policy will help improve the quality and returns of your business. Here are some basic steps you can follow to make certain you have an adequate risk program in place:

1. Have a business plan.

2. Go over your business plan and identify each area that could involve risk.

3. Take time to know your business. Imagine all possible catastrophes that could occur.

4. Decide what action or coverage is needed to handle that possibility.

5. For risks that are covered by insurance, determine how much and what type is needed.

6. Choose an insurance to cover those risks.

7. Get quotes on the insurance you need.

8. Arrange for insurance coverage to begin before you open your business.

9. For risks that are not covered by insurance, put together a contingency plan for handling the identified risks.

10. Train employees so they are prepared should any of these emergencies arise.

11. Put your plan in a place where it can be accessed quickly if needed.

12. Review your plan annually.

Risk assessment

Risks can originate from a number of difference sources. Some may be obvious and can be identified prior to project start, others are identifiable during its life cycle, and some are identified by anyone associated with the project. Some risks are inherent to the project itself, while others are influenced by external influences that are completely outside your control.

Risk assessment determines which of these risks are likely to affect your business and may involve some of these elements:

- Description of the risk factor or event, e.g., design errors, omissions, weather, delays, etc.

- Probability that the risk will occur. This can be measured in a probability percentage of 1% to 100%. Zero probability poses no threat, while 100% probability means that the risk has already occurred.

- Schedule impact risks, which involves the number of hours, days, weeks, or months that could affect your schedule and timetable.

- Scope impact, which envisions the impact said risks will have on your business.

- Quality impact, which envisions a reduction in the quality of work or products that are being developed.

- Cost impact, which envisions the effect the risks will have on the budget.

Risk mitigation

Once you have identified a risk, a response should be identified with it. This usually involves determining the degree to which the actions to mitigate the risk are taken.

One way of evaluating mitigation strategies is to multiply the risk cost times the probability of it happening again. Risk mitigation strategies involve two steps:

- Identifying various activities or steps to reduce the probability and impact of the risk

- Creation of a contingency plan to deal with the risk

Risk contingency planning

This involves preparing a plan, including a series of activities you can do to manage the risk, if it occurs. Having a contingency plan helps you think in advance of a course of action if a risk event takes place. A contingency plan should include the following:

1. Tasks or steps taken to implement the mitigation strategy

2. Identify resources such as money, equipment and labor

3. The contingency plan schedule. Since it is unknown when the plan is going to be implemented, the schedule will be in the format of day 1, day 2, day 3, etc.

4. Define emergency notification and escalation procedures

5. Develop contingency plan training materials

The contingency plan should be reviewed and updated when necessary. After the plan is outlined and reviewed, a copy should be distributed to management and those directly involved in executing the plans. It may also be advisable that you set aside a budget for your contingency plan. The amount of budget for contingency is generally limited to high probability risks.

Insuring against risks

Taking out an insurance policy is an important part of risk management. When you take out insurance you hedge against any losses by transferring it to another entity in exchange for a premium. This is basic risk management as it helps protect not only your business but your loved ones in the event of accidents, death, or the loss of the ability to work.

The four main types of insurance are general insurance, private health insurance, personal insurance and business insurance. Each will be discussed in greater detail in this chapter.

General Insurance

General Insurance covers an insurance which is not determined as life insurance. It covers home insurance, contents insurance and motor vehicle insurance.

- Home insurance is designed to provide financial protection against damages/loss to your home.

- Contents insurance provides financial protection against damages to contents inside your home. Most homeowners have a combined home and contents policy. If you are renting, a separate contents policy may be appropriate.

- Motor Vehicle Insurance covers three areas:

1. Comprehensive car insurance which covers damages to your own vehicle as well as any damages you may cause to the property of others.

2. Third party property which protects you against damage claims your car causes to another person's vehicle or property.

3. Compulsory third party (CTP) which protects the owner and driver of the motor vehicle in the event of a personal injury claim. It does not cover damages to property or other vehicles.

Private Health Insurance

This type of insurance offers an incentive for individuals who have private health insurance to a 30% tax offset (commonly known as a rebate.) All Australians who pay for health insurance may claim this rebate.

In April 2005, the Government amended the provisions of the private health insurance incentive schemes to benefit older Australians. These amendments increased the rebate from 30% to 35% for policies covering at least one person aged 65 years to 69 years, and to 40% for policies covering at least one person aged 70 and older.

Personal Insurance

There are four main types of personal insurance:

Term Life (or Death): This insurance pays a lump sum benefit on the death of the insured. Term life insurance enables beneficiaries to do the following: repay debts, cover capital gains tax liabilities that may arise from the settling of the estate, cover dependents for the loss of the income provider, and secure a business interest. Under this scheme, premiums are generally non-tax deductible, and the proceeds are paid to beneficiaries as untaxed income.

Total and Permanent Disablement (TPD): TPD is a stand-alone benefit generally included in a term life insurance policy. It provides a lump sum payment in cases where the policy-holder suffers a permanent illness or injury. The coverage can apply to any occupation regardless of education, training or experience. TPD premiums are generally non-tax deductible, and proceeds are exempt from income tax depending on the circumstances under which the policy was taken out and who owns it.

Trauma, Critical Illness, or Living Insurance: This policy offers a lump sum payment for holders who suffer a specified major health trauma, including certain cancers, heart disorders, nervous system disorders, various accident conditions, specific body organ disorders, and loss of speech.

Generally, trauma insurance covers the gaps in the effect of other insurances. If a policy holder, for example, suffers a mild heart attack but is able to return to work after two months they are not covered by term life insurance, as they are still alive. They do not qualify for TPD coverage, as they are able to work again. They may be encumbered, however, by large medical bills, or may have a need to change their working habits to stay healthy.

In this situation, trauma insurance becomes valuable since it pays out on the actual occurrence of the incident. Premiums are generally non-tax deductible and the proceeds are paid tax-free. An exception occurs where the trauma insurance is part of a key person insurance policy.

Income Protection, Sickness and Accident, or Salary Continuance Insurance: Most working people depend on their income to provide for themselves and their family, which makes the ability to earn an income their most valuable asset. Thus, it becomes important to have this income insured against unforeseen circumstances. Income protection insurance covers up to 75% of policy holder's annual taxable income if they become unable to work because of sickness or injury. Premiums for this type of policy are generally tax deductible. Any proceeds received from this policy are considered assessable income for income tax purposes.

Business Insurance

Business liability insurance covers business operations and cash flow stability. It protects total and partial business liabilities, shareholders and/or partners' loans; provides sufficient cash to clear or reduce liabilities as well as cover joint and several liabilities of business guarantors. Business insurance comes in many forms:

1. *Business liability protection*

   Is an insurance that provides the business with sufficient cash to clear or reduce business liabilities and covers joint and several liabilities of business guarantors. This insurance protects the total and partial liabilities of the business, shareholders and/or partners' loans, and guarantees provided.

2. *Key person insurance*

   This insurance protects a business in the event of the loss of a principal or employee who makes a significant contribution toward the profitability and stability of the business. Key person insurance provides the business with sufficient cash to cover the replacement of key employees, implement appropriate restructuring arrangements, and protect against loss of future profits. Key person insurance policies usually cover the sole trader (yourself or your spouse), other partners or joint owners, the principal owner of a one-person company, employees or directors, and/or a key person outside of the business.

3. *Partner/shareholder Protection*

   This insurance provides the surviving partner(s)/ shareholder(s) with sufficient cash to acquire the disabled or deceased partner's share in the business. It is intended to ensure that a disabled partner or the estate of a deceased partner receives a fair and equitable dollar value for their share in the business. It will provide for loss of future income for the disabled partner or his/her estate, cover any capital gains tax payable by the estate upon the sale of shares, and provide a lump sum in the event of a major trauma.

4. *Income protection for business owners*

This insurance will provide up to 75% of the regular monthly income for business principals or employees should they become disabled and unable to work as a result of sickness or injury. Benefits are paid monthly in line with the waiting period (14, 30, 90 or 720 days) and benefit period (2 years, 5 years, or to age 65) selected. There is usually a choice of agreed benefit or indemnity options available. Premiums are paid by the individuals or business, and the policy is generally owned by the insured party. Premiums are deductible and proceeds are assessable.

5. *Business overheads protection*

This insurance covers the day-to-day costs of running a business for up to 12 months in the event of a business principal becoming disabled and unable to work in the business as a result of sickness or injury.

Benefits are paid monthly in line with the selected waiting period (14 or 30 days), and paid for a fixed period up to 12 months. Premiums are paid by the business, and are tax deductible and assessable upon distribution.

Using superannuation to pay for some of your insurance obligations

You can look to use your super to pay for some of these insurances. This is a great strategy as it allows these essential components of a wealth protection strategy to be paid for by your super and NOT your cash flow. Note however that you must be creating wealth in other ways and not relying solely on your super. Paying for your insurances via super will reduce the ability of your super to maximise its returns.

Do you know what you can afford to lose? For a FREE no obligation financial assessment, contact a team member of Acquire Wealth Solutions today on 1300 734 647.

In this FREE assessment you will learn:

- How to insure what you cannot afford to lose without it costing a cent out of your weekly cash flow

- What types of insurances you definitely cannot do without

- Learn about which insurances you need, when you need them

Most people think 'she'll be right mate!' The problem is that this is not the case. If you think you do not need insurances... think again!

The most common claim was for cancer. The most common age for trauma claims were in the 50 to 59 age group. 14% of the claims were from people aged 30 to 39.

Did you know that 64% of death claims were from males? Imagine what this would do to your family if it happened to you. Could your wife afford the mortgage or pay for your kid's education and upbringing?

Did you know that between the age of 40 and 79, 68% of us will be dead?

STEP - 4

Superannuation

Attitudes are contagious.
Make yours worth catching.

~ Unknown

Superannuation (otherwise known as super) helps you save money that you can later use during retirement, or if an illness renders you temporarily unable to work, or a small nest egg you can bequeath your loved ones upon your death.

In Australia, super begins when people start to work and once their employers start paying for them. Super funds are usually managed by trustees. Though each has its own rules, it remains subject to government regulations, which are designed to ensure it is properly managed.

Employer contributions

Employers are required to start paying super once an employee becomes eligible, which means they must be aged between 18 and under 70 years; and if they have been paid at least $450 (before tax) in a calendar month. If the employee is under 18, they become eligible if they meet the additional requirement of working more than 30 hours a week.

As an employer, your superannuation guarantee obligations include:

- Pay a minimum of 9% of an employee's earnings into a super account each quarter

- Pay the superannuation guarantee charge to the Tax Office if you failed to pay the contributions by the due dates

- Check if any of your employees are eligible for a choice of super fund.

- Provide your eligible employees with a standard choice form

- Pass on your employees' tax file numbers to their super fund

- Pay super contributions for your contractors

- Keep records of your super contribution payments

There are two types of superannuation contributions:

Concessional contributions

These are generally contributions your employer makes, including amounts you pay to super, and contributions you make and claim as an income tax deduction. Concessional contributions are tax deductible and usually taxed 15% in the Super Fund although there are some exceptions.

Concessional caps

You can contribute up to $50,000 into your super account each year. If you go over that cap, you pay an additional 31.5% extra tax on the contributions amount. If you are aged 50 or more during a transitional financial year (2011-12), your concessional contribution cap for that year will be about $100,000.

Non-concessional contributions

These are contributions you make from your own money and for which you can't claim a tax deduction. Non-concessional contributions are also called after-tax contributions, un-deducted contributions or personal contributions. Your fund does not pay any tax on your non-concessional contributions, nor can you claim a tax deduction.

Sources of non-concessional contributions usually come from your take home net pay, your savings, your business profits or money from selling an asset, an inheritance you received, the tax-free portion of any foreign super that you transfer to your Australian super account and any contributions in excess of your concessional contributions cap.

Spouse contributions are also classified under the non-concessional contributions. Spouse contributions (up to a maximum $3000) usually receive an 18% tax offset to the contributing spouse if the eligibility criteria are met, that is, if you earn $13,800 or less in a financial year. The super contributions your spouse puts into your fund will also be tax-free when you withdraw them at retirement.

Non-concessional caps

Unlike its concessional counterpart, you are allowed to make up to $ 150,000 a year in non-concessional contributions. You can also bring forward some of your contributions if you are aged under 65 in a financial year. Instead of a yearly cap of $150,000, your contribution can go as high as $450,000 over a three-year period - but with certain conditions. Also, if you go over the non-concessional contribution cap, you are required to pay 46.5% extra on tax over the concession cap.

Self-employed contributions

If you are self-employed, the law does not require you to contribute to a super fund. However, you may wish to use the fund as a hedge against retirement and for tax deduction purposes.

If you are considering using super as a form of retirement savings, just ensure that your chosen super fund is one that complies with all government regulations.

Self-employed people are generally eligible for the super co-contribution which took effect in July 2007. You can receive the super co-contribution only if 10% or more of your income comes from eligible employment, running a business or both.

Types of superannuation funds

There are different types of superannuation funds, which can be categorised into two broad categories: profit funds for the members (retail superannuation funds) and profit funds for the owners (industry super funds).

There are many debates as to which fund category is better so it is important to understand the key differences and the funds' advantages and disadvantages. The following are the main types of superannuation funds investors may want to join:

Retail super funds

These funds are run by financial institutions and are open for investment to the general public. The master trust is the most popular super fund within the retail superannuation. Master trusts pool accounts for investment and have single corporate trustees and trust deeds that allow individuals and companies to participate. Master trusts are offered to the public by fund companies and banks, and operate as investment platforms. These trusts are characterised by a broad range of multi-manager and single sector investment options which are managed by leading fund managers.

Advantages

Investors can take full advantage of the tax concessions of investing inside the super. Also, master trusts offer benefits such as death, total and permanent disability, and salary continuance which are often provided by related life insurance companies.

Disadvantages

Fees associated with the master trusts. Since retail super funds pay adviser commissions, investors could be paying entry/ contribution fees on each contribution as well as commission fees, especially if the fund was set up with an advisor.

Corporate super funds

These are generally only open to people working for a particular corporation. In some organisations, membership is made available to ex-employees or relatives of existing employees.

Employers are required by law to offer a default super fund option for employees as an alternative to exercising Choice of Fund rights for those who do not wish to choose their own super fund. Corporate super funds can be set up through retail master trusts or employers can choose to operate their own employer-sponsored super funds.

Advantage

Depending on their size, corporate super funds can enjoy a number of benefits. Large organisations can negotiate lower special fee arrangements while accessing the same or similar range of investment options.

Disadvantage

Corporate super funds are limited as they are only available for people working at the organisation. This means that if you cease employment with the company, you may no longer be able to contribute to the fund.

Retirement savings account (RSAs)

RSAs are accounts offered by banks, building societies, credit unions, life insurance companies and prescribed financial institutions. Capital guaranteed and similar to superannuation funds, RSAs operate much like bank accounts, except where restrictions apply on withdrawals.

Advantage

RSAs are low-risk products and have lower levels of fees and charges. In most cases, they also include death and disability insurance benefits.

Disadvantage

Since super savings are invested in bank deposits, they pay lower interest rates than regular super funds, which, in turn, results in lower rates of returns.

Profit for member funds

In contrast, profit for member funds deliver profits to its members instead of shareholders. Profit for member funds generally are made available to employers working for particular industries.

Industry funds

These multi-employer funds are usually operated by industrial parties like employer associations and unions. Services are offered to members of a specific industry, such as retail and hospitality workers, builders, etc.

Advantage

Rather than being paid to shareholders, all profits are returned to members' accounts. No commissions are involved as the fund does not employ any financial advisor.

Disadvantage

Investment options are limited to a small selection of available investment options. In contrast to the 100+ multi-and-single sector options available to retail investors, industry funds are usually limited to 10 multi-sector investments options.

Self-managed funds

Also known as DIY super funds, self-managed super funds can have up to four members and are generally established by an individual or a family from their own superannuation savings. Unless a corporate trustee is appointed, members also act as trustees, and are responsible for all investment and compliance decisions of the fund, which include administration, trusteeship and taxation.

Advantage

Since you manage your own super fund, it can offer greater control and access to a broader range of investment options such as shares, direct property, and alternative asset classes that are not available to conventional super funds.

Disadvantage

These can become costly to run. Since members are responsible for their decisions, it may create conflicts later on especially where legislative compliance is concerned. SMSF cannot invest in businesses so they may not be appropriate for all business people.

Public sector funds

Public sector funds provide superannuation for employees in the public sector, which are run and structured with the same benefits as industry funds. They also include funds established for public servants, for employees of statutory authorities and local government.

In Australia, the Commonwealth government has set up statutory superannuation funds for its public servants like the Commonwealth Superannuation Scheme, the Public Sector Superannuation Scheme and the Military Superannuation and Benefits Scheme. The schemes provide generous death and invalidity benefits and may also allow salary continuance insurance cover.

Super is an important part of any wealth creation plan. Along with your FREE insurance review, take advantage of a super review as well!

What you will learn from this financial assessment:

- Why choosing the wrong super can cost you thousands

- How to have more control of your super without doing it yourself

- How to consolidate your super to reduce fees

- How to borrow for property using your super

- Self-managed super funds (SMSF) - are they all they're cracked up to be?

Superannuation is one of the best ways to help you legally reduce your taxes and protect your wealth. In some cases your creditors (people you owe money to) cannot touch your super.

You must find out what you can do with your super. Do not delay; make use of this financial assessment NOW!

Call 1300 734 647 for your
FREE 20 min phone consultation!

Stop the press. With the Cooper's report now out it is even more important to contact us to find out what the changes really mean to you.

STEP - 5

Estate Planning

By working faithfully eight hours a day, you may eventually get to be boss and work twelve hours a day.

~ Robert Frost

Estate planning is more than just writing a well-drafted Will. It also involves preparing the Will, appointing an executor, determining whether a power of attorney is necessary (and who should have that power,) and establishing a discretionary (or testamentary) trust or trusts if the situation warrants.

Estate planning involves all the assets you own or control. It also provides for any follow-on effects after your death such as instances when you guaranteed a loan or you get married. Although a Will is an important component of any estate plan, it is unlikely to be the only transfer mechanism involved.

What is a Will?

A Will is a legal statement by which you name the people you want to receive your property and possessions when you die.

Why should everyone make a Will?

- Making a Will is the surest way anyone has of providing for others after their death. You may think that you are not wealthy enough. But stop to add up the value of your house, car, savings, and insurance policies - the total is probably more than you realised.

- A Will is particularly important for anyone with a family or other dependents, especially if you are a separated or unmarried parent.

- A Will enables you to ensure that the people to whom you give your property receive it promptly and in a manner which will render your estate free of liability to, or at least little liability to, additional income tax through capital gains tax. Capital gains tax liabilities may be postponed rather than provoked by appropriate provisions in your will.

- A Will enables you to choose your executor, i.e. the person who will manage and distribute your property.

- All too often, leaving no Will creates yet another worry for your family at the time of bereavement and disruption at home. Making a Will is a way of making life easier for them.

Who can make a Will?

If you are of sound mind and at least eighteen years of age, you can make a Will. A Will made by a person under the age of eighteen is not valid unless he or she is or has been married or the Court grants leave to make a Will in terms disclosed to the Court, or the Will is made in contemplation of a marriage on the solemnisation of which the Will becomes valid.

What is a valid Will?

A valid Will is one that will be accepted by a Court and is able to be put into effect. To be valid, your Will must be:

- In writing - handwritten, typed or printed

- Signed - ideally your signature should be at the end of the Will

- Witnessed - two witnesses must be present when you sign the Will and they must also sign at the end of the document. You must all be together when the Will is being signed and witnessed. If your Will is not drawn up in this manner it may not be enforceable and your property could be disposed of as if you had not made a Will at all. The Court has a discretion to grant or not grant probate (confirm that the Will is valid) if your Will is not drawn up in the correct way. The Court needs to be satisfied that the document represents your testamentary intentions.

What happens if I don't make one?

Then your property will be distributed according to a rigid formula. The formula may not distribute the property in the way you would have wanted. Your children, or other minors in your care, may not receive the protection you would have desired. Incapacitated members of your family and their own assets may be put at risk. Furthermore, if you do not leave a Will, the legal procedures are more complicated and time consuming. This may cause expense, worry and even hardship to your family. It is not true that the government takes a deceased person's property if there is no Will. This only happens in exceptional circumstances where there is no close relatives or persons in a family relationship surviving the deceased.

Once a Will is made, how do I ensure that it is carried out?

You must appoint a person or persons, who are willing to handle your estate after you die, as 'Executors' to administer the distribution of your property. Any adult person can act as Executor; your spouse, child, friend, or solicitor. Naturally, it should be established that this person is competent, trustworthy and is prepared to accept the task. A beneficiary can also be the Executor.

Usually, the Executor manages and distributes the estate with the assistance of a solicitor.

Can I alter my Will if I change my mind?

Yes. You are free to alter your Will at any time. It is in your interest to review your Will every two to three years or whenever any major event occurs in your family, your assets or the taxation laws to make sure the Will is up to date and still meets your requirements. However, you cannot make an alteration by, for instance, crossing something out on the original Will and writing in your new wishes. If the alterations are minor, you can make a Codicil (this is a separate document in which you change a provision in your Will) but it is better to make an entirely new Will. A Codicil must be signed in the presence of two witnesses, in the same way you drew up your original Will.

How does marriage affect an existing Will?

If you made up a Will before you married, it will automatically be revoked when you marry, unless it was expressly made in contemplation of the particular marriage, not just marriage in general. So, if you marry, it is more than likely you will need to draw up a new Will.

How will divorce affect my Will?

Any gift or appointment in favour of a former spouse in your Will is automatically revoked when a divorce decree becomes absolute, but this is not the case if you are only separated. It is in your best interest to make a new Will if you are divorced.

Can anyone challenge my Will?

Yes, under the Family Provision legislation, the main concept of which is that close members of the deceased's family and his dependents (for example a spouse or child) who are left without adequate provision in a Will may apply to the Court for further provision out of the estate.

Where should I keep my Will?

In a safe, secure place, such as with your solicitor or your bank. You should keep a copy of your Will at home and note on it where the original is kept. It is advisable to tell your Executor where your Will is kept.

How can a solicitor help me?

Your solicitor will:

- Make sure your Will is valid; that it is properly drawn, signed and witnessed

- Make sure your wishes are clearly expressed in the Will

- Advise on the making of adequate provision for your spouse and children or for any former spouse or dependents and thereby minimise any challenges to your Will

- Advise you as to any possible liability for capital gains tax which might result from the provisions you intend to make in your Will; advise you on choosing an Executor

- Advise you on the best way to arrange your affairs to provide a suitable balance between enjoyment of property and income during life, and the preservation or creation of capital for your family, or other beneficiaries upon death

- Keep the Will in a safe place for you.

In general, solicitors do not charge a large fee for making a Will. As a Will is one of the most important legal documents you will ever make, it is a false economy to try to do it without skilled, professional advice.

Why you need estate planning

You need estate planning to avoid dying intestate. Dying intestate means that you died without having executed a valid Will, which provides instructions for passing your estate on to your heirs. If you die intestate, the State will dictate how your estate will be administered. If you have no surviving heirs, your assets will be taken by the State. In other words, if you die intestate your assets might pass to a beneficiary you may not have wanted to benefit in the first place.

One way to manage your bequests is to use a trust. The trust provides for the estate to be taken safely over some of these financial risks, which include:

Probate

Your estate goes on a probate process when you die intestate. Probate handles two major functions for your estate: (1) it identifies the rightful heirs to your estate and the share size each heir will receive; (2) it takes the legal title of the property out of your name and into the name of your rightful heirs.

The first function would have been taken care of if you made a Will in advance of your death. Without a valid Will, the State will use its own formula for determining your heirs and their share. But even with a Will, the re-titling of your estate still has to go through a probate procedure. Avoiding probate then is desirable since it can be a very expensive process that can see a large part of your estate go to the government. In some cases, probates can also drag on for years, which can lead to family battles, loss of privacy and your wishes not being completely satisfied.

You can avoid probate if you set up a family estate planning trust, which can be either a living trust or a life estate trust. A trust avoids probate by titling your property in the name of the trust before your death. You control the property during your life but it becomes the property of the trust when you die. Your pre-selected trustee then simply handles the transfers or payments to your specified heirs upon your death without lawyers, court supervision, or excessive costs.

Joint tenancy ownership

Joint tenancy ownership grants a right of survivorship. In other words, the deceased joint tenant's former interest in the asset does not follow the direction of the Will. Immediately following the death of one person who has an interest in a particular asset, all other joint tenants instantly and equally share in and become owners of that asset.

This approach does work as a probate avoidance technique.

But there may be some potential problems:

- Since the whole amount of the estate is held in joint tenancy, all of the liabilities are shouldered by the joint owners. If one owner gets a judgment, the property can be taken to satisfy the judgment. If a parent holds a home in joint tenancy with a child and that child divorces, the divorcing spouse of the child can sue the property as a divorce settlement.

- If the property owner is survived by a spouse, this surviving spouse has outright control of the assets. The danger is that if this surviving spouse gets remarried, he/she may give some of these assets away, cutting the original heirs out of the estate.

- If the surviving spouse doesn't do any estate planning, then probate could be inevitable on this second death.

Beneficiary arrangements

Many assets can be successfully transferred to heirs through beneficiary arrangements like pension plans, insurance policies, annuities, and bank and investment accounts. Upon the death of the original owner, the death benefits are paid quickly to the named beneficiaries without probate. The system, however, has problems and limitations:

- There are no controlled or timed payouts to the beneficiaries

- There are no provisions for beneficiaries incapable of handling their financial affairs

- Beneficiary contributions can be subjected to lawsuits, liens, bankruptcies, and divorce problems of the beneficiary

- If the beneficiary predeceases the original owner, the money is paid to the spouse of the beneficiary instead of being held or paid to the beneficiary's children

Incapacitation

If the property owner who has sole or joint tenancy ownership becomes mentally incapacitated, the property goes into legal limbo. The property then cannot be sold or even leased. In most cases, the answer is to have an expensive and time delaying court conservatorship procedure. Aside from a family trust, the best way to comprehensively deal with incapacitation issues is a simple device known as a durable power of attorney.

The importance of estate planning

The lack of estate planning can leave benefactors in a vulnerable position. Known simply as asset protection, estate planning uses a special type of family trust to deal with the problems of probate, taxes and other risks that can, in the long run, harm the value of your estate.

One of the most harmful attacks on your estate is the back-breaking taxes your heirs may be subjected to upon your death. Taxes diminish the value of your estate, which means that your heirs may not receive your assets with a basis which is equal to its original fair market value. And when your heirs sell those assets, they may also be required to pay capital gains taxes on the gain (profit).

The bottom line is this: if you have a net worth of $1 million by the time of your death, then your estate faces death taxation issues. This is where estate planning comes in.

With good estate planning, you can easily increase 'death tax'* exemptions by several million dollars. Some type of trust, however, is required for maximum reduction of death taxation since neither a will, beneficiary arrangements nor joint tenancy ownership are sufficient to take care of death taxation issues for either married or single estate owners.

* Death tax was abolished in Australia in 1981. When we refer to death tax here we refer collectively to capital gains tax and stamp duties that can occur after death.

Estate transfer and heir planning

One of the big benefits of pre-death estate planning is the ability to name your heirs, specify their share in your estate, and dictate the manner and timing they should get their inheritance. This part of estate planning actually can be done with either a Will or a trust.

Heir planning is also an important part of estate planning. But there are issues that must be considered if you're planning your heir. Some of these include:

1. Whether your heirs are to receive equal or unequal shares

2. What age the heirs should be to get their share and/ or whether these shares are to be paid in installments at different age milestones, or paid out in full

3. Whether or not to leave specific property to certain heirs

4. Whether to disinherit any heirs

5. Solving a situation where a married couple have children from other relationships but they want to create one comprehensive estate plan

6. Dealing with cases where estate owners get married after building their own separate estate, which they may want their new spouse to benefit from but not their spouse's heirs

7. Dealing with cases where a child has a health issue and the parents fear that the child will misuse the inheritance

8. Dealing with mentally or physically disabled heirs.

9. What happens when an heir predeceases the estate owner.

10. Dealing with specific gifts to special heirs e.g. grandchildren, the wedding rings to the eldest grand-daughter, etc.

Trusts vs. Wills, which is best for you?

In most cases, a Will is used under the following circumstances:

*   If the estate is small enough not to need a formal probate; if the estate has no significant death taxation liabilities;

*   If there is no need to hold an heir's share in some type of scheduled or controlled payout;

*   If the estate owner's mental incapacitation will not cause financial or legal problems after his death.

Whatever the case may be, everyone should have a Will regardless of the amount of money involved.

Types of Wills

There are four types of Wills which address different categories or needs. They are:

*   The standard Will,

*   The standard tax effective Will,

*   The commercial tax effective Will, and

*   The asset protection Will.

This book will focus primarily on the asset protection Will.

Asset protection Wills are tailored to ensure that your assets remain within your family or with your lineal descendants for up to 80 years after your death. The level of asset protection can be structured to it your particular circumstances and address your concerns in regards to business creditors, bankruptcy, divorce proceedings, social security asset issues, or legal actions that may adversely affect your beneficiaries.

Specific instructions for completion of background information related to an asset protection can be found in Appendix 5.

A Will is likely to be the best choice when:

1. The estate is worth less than $50,000 then joint tenancy and beneficiary arrangements may apply. If one of the spouses dies the survivor may live many more years and can provide all the best possible care for minor children.

2. The Will handles the disposition of personal effects. The will serves as a catch-all in the event there are assets you forgot about, received after the Will was prepared, or there is a problem or mistake with a beneficiary or joint tenancy arrangement.

Reviewing your Will

There are a number of reasons why you need to review the provisions in your Will and your estate plan in general:

- When you get married or divorced

- The birth or adoption of a child

- The death of a family member or other beneficiary of your estate

- When an individual named as executor, trustee, or guardian dies or is unable to act as such

- When you decide to name someone else as your executor, trustee, or guardian

Review your Will if:

- The size of your estate changes significantly

- You move to another state

- There are changes in federal or state laws that could affect your estate

In addition, there have been significant and continuous changes regarding superannuation, taxation and social security laws' impact on Wills and deceased estates in recent years. These changes emphasise the importance of regularly reviewing your Will to ensure that it continues to comply with your wishes.

Revising your Will

If you want to revise your Will, there are three ways you can do it:

- By preparing an amendment called a 'codicil.' A codicil needs to be executed with all the formalities required for signing a Will but need not restate all of the unchanged provisions in the Will.

- By preparing a new Will revoking the prior Will or by destroying the old Will. Care must be taken when destroying a Will to avoid intestacy.

- By independent events such as divorce or adoption. In certain states, a divorce automatically revokes any bequest to the former spouse. In other states, laws provide that a divorce revokes the Will entirely. A new Will should be prepared in order to remove the spouse as a beneficiary and/or fiduciary. The beneficiary designations on life insurance policies and retirement benefits should also be reviewed.

Trusts

As stated in the previous chapter, a trust is a device used to take care of property in special ways. It is created between two parties as a legal agreement, basically a contract. Known as the appointor and the trustee, these parties create the agreement for the benefit of a third party, the beneficiary.

The executor/trustee

An executor or trustee is the person responsible for carrying out all your wishes in your Will or Trust. It is advisable that you designate both a primary and alternate executor as a precaution in the event your primary executor may be unable to perform his/her duties. If your primary trustee dies while executing your estate and you did not designate an alternate executor, it will be left up to the Court to appoint one.

It is also possible that although this person may have great interest in your Will he/she may not act according to your wishes.

The main rule in appointing a trustee or executor is to appoint someone whom you trust. The executor does not need to invest assets other than on a temporary basis, but the major role of the trustee is to prudently invest the trust assets so as to be fair to all of the beneficiaries. The role of an executor has a limited duration while a trustee may serve for many generations.

If your Will requires a trustee to maintain a business, the powers granted under current State or Territory Trustee Act laws may be inadequate. In order to afford maximum flexibility in today's dynamic commercial environment, you can avoid this potential problem by formulating a set of specific 'expanded powers' for your trustees and executors.

A trust is useful in the following circumstances:

1. The estate exceeds the amount of $450,000 and is non-ransferrable through beneficiary or joint tenancy arrangements.

2. The estate could be challenged by an heir or would-be heir. Generally, a trust can withstand these challenges better than probate and for less money and hassle.

3. The estate cannot immediately pay outright to one or more heirs since there are minor heirs awaiting their shares to be paid in a controlled or scheduled manner.

4. Significant death taxation liabilities.

5. There is a need to insulate assets from legal difficulties and claims following a divorce.

STEP - 6

Mindset

If you want your dreams to come true,
the first thing you have to do is wake up.

~ J.M. Power

If you do not have the correct mindset you will never keep your wealth. The stats on lotto winners losing all their winnings are staggering. It's something like 94%. That's right: 94% who win large amounts of money end up with less than they had before they won the lottery! So, how do you keep first what you have, then build on and keep wealth? There are so many books, MP3s and seminars, how can I do it all, you ask?

It all comes down to mind set. I'm going to take myself as an example right now. I look back at what I have done to change my mind set and the following is what stands out the most:

1. Read

They say certain books will choose you when you need them. I remember when I was about 16 I picked up the book *Think and Grow Rich* by Napoleon Hill. I tried to read it, however, I never finished it. Twenty years later, I picked it up again and I read it in one night. I constantly go back to it and re-read it over and over - it's my original mind set book where I feel most others are based on this one book. Others that have helped me along the way are *How to Win Friends and Influence People* by Dale Carnegie,

7 Habits of Highly Successful People by Stephen Covey, Your Life, Your Legacy by Roger Hamilton, and *The Power of One* by Bryce Courtney. I have read hundreds of books over the years and the list would go for pages and pages. The ones above though will give you a good foundation to get your mind set on the right path.

2. Dream / meditate

Dreaming and meditation are one and the same, but are still different. How? The answer will depend on who you talk to. I love to dream and dream big, and daydreaming is part of it. If you are a parent, I urge you to let your kids dream. The bigger they dream, the better.

Dreaming or visualising what you want was made 'hip' in the movie *The Secret.* I don't actually care how it works; all I know is that it does. If you want to acquire wealth, then start by visualising it. Visualise yourself making tons of money; visualise total financial abundance flowing toward you. It does exist. You only need to tap into it to get it.

While visualising, cancel out any negative thoughts. Guard your mind against negative ideas. Think only of great ideas because if you do, you'll get great results.

Monitor your internal dialogue and what other people are saying to you, especially regarding money matters. If they're dead broke, run away as fast as you can. If they're wealthy, stay, listen and learn.

Meditation helps me get centred, quiets my mind and helps me focus on, well, me. I don't want to drag on here, because I could talk about meditation all day, but I will ask you to give it a try. Wealthy people take time out every day for themselves. Some great meditation tracks I have listened to are from Doreen Virtue, Centerpoint, and Sacred Earth.

3. Write your goals down

We think millions of thoughts, and every day, pieces of data run through our minds like a memory card. Writing your goals down helps keep you focused on what is important and helps them become real. There are several ways you can write them down. First do the SMART assessment, which stands for Specific, Measurable, Attainable, Relevant, and Time-Bound.

Then start towards acquiring the unique traits that many wealthy and successful people have in common:

1. Clear and concise

2. Realistic

3. Ecological

4. As now

5. Time

6. End state

Christopher Howard uses the CREATE method and it is the one I use the most.

4. Listen

I listen to a lot of MP3s. Having an iPod and iPhone have made it easier to carry lots of music and self-help audios. Some of my collection include: Dale Carnegie, Brian Tracy, Robert Kiyosaki, and Abraham Hicks. Use your time wisely.

Whether you're on a train, bus or just stuck in traffic, control what you're listening to. The wealthy do this very well.

5. Mentor

I found that when I started to ask people to mentor me, my wealth (and business) increased in speed. Having someone to hold you accountable can make a big difference in your success. I am always eternally grateful to my past, present and future mentors.

6. Take action

Taking action is like saying you are not afraid to fail. Failing is about guiding you in the right direction. It's no good having the best ideas in the world if you do not act on them - and remember, a good plan executed now is better than a great plan executed later. Do not be afraid to fail because failing can help steer you in the right direction. I think Nike says it best: *Just do it.*

7. Focus

My friends and colleagues laughed when they read this part of the book. Why? Well, I struggle to focus. I am always looking at this deal and that deal; starting that, never finishing this. One of the biggest mistakes I made starting out was not focusing on what is required to complete something I started. I got bored. Quite often, I found something that worked and stopped doing it. Yes, you read that correctly.

I found something that worked and stopped doing it. Now I know that I can focus on three projects at one time. Less than three and I get bored. More than three and things can go wrong or nothing gets finished. Work out your focus level and stay within it.

8. Watch

Choose carefully what you watch, whether it's on TV or at the movies. Again, take control over what goes into your brain. One of the best movies I have seen is The Secret. I also like Star Wars and Lord of the Rings. I am not saying to stop watching TV altogether, just limit it somewhat. Cut out the news for example, because processing too many negative and disturbing visions every day can't be good for you - better if you miss it altogether.

9. Time out for yourself

Have you ever heard of the 5 O'clock Club or the 6 O'clock Club? Sometimes, to get a bit of time to yourself you need to get up earlier than you are used to. This habit has definitely helped me towards achieving success.

10. Participate

Get out, go to seminars. Seminars have probably been the biggest part in helping me shift my mind set.

I remember once in September 2006, I went to a Christopher Howard Breakthrough to Success seminar. It was like nothing

I had ever been to. Over those three days, I laughed, cried, hugged complete strangers.

What happened was that something inside me changed and I started to see things in a different light. I started to think bigger, act differently, attract bigger and better opportunities. Try something new, learn something new.

No matter what you do, successful people take action. They do not dwell on the 'what if'. They just do it. So take action today.

Action, Action, Action!!!!

DO YOU WANT TO SUCCEED IN BUSINESS?

If so ... then this is for you.

Mark Robinson has created his very own The Law of Success in Business Mastery program. Mark will only take a limited number of business owners every year and one of the graduates will get it for FREE. That's right if you fully complete his program, not only will he guarantee your profits and life balance will increase, the student who shows the most dedication and desire to succeed will be fully refunded their tuition fee.

Our program is 100% backed by our money back guarantee.

What will be covered in this program?

- The 17 Laws of success that Napoleon Hill spent 25 years researching

- Business planning

- Sales training

- Marketing, with a FREE website creation

- Systemising your business ready to sell and/or duplicate

- Lead generation using the internet

- Networking

- 100 ready-made templates for all areas of your business from policy and procedures manual to HR forms, hiring and firing procedures etc. all done for you

- Become an expert in your niche. I will give you the recipe to create your own book

- Access to my black book of contacts for web design, lead generation, marketing, copy writers and many more ...

- My personal library of self-help books, MP3s and videos

This is no teleconference or group round table. The best part is that this program allows you direct access to Mark and his team. You will receive up to ten full days with Mark and his team over the twelve months. No other coaching program does that.

Hurry there are only eleven spaces for this life changing course. This course has been valued at over $47k. A special launch price of only $35997 paid monthly.

Yes! Mark I want to sign up for your Law of success in business mastery program. I understand that I will need to commit 12 months of my life to this and that I may be lucky enough to get this for FREE.

My Guarantee

I also understand that if you do not keep your promise and that I implement your program fully and for some reason it does not work I will be able to receive a full refund.

Tear this page out and post it to us or scan and email or just ring us today. I know this program will not last.

Post to: PO Box 648 Moffat Beach Qld 4551

Email to: mark@acquiregroup.com.au - or call 1300 734 647

PS: I will be opening my black book of contacts to ensure you have everything you need to succeed. I will be providing you with every tool I have come across over my 20 odd years in business. You WILL succeed in my program - I personally guarantee it!

STEP - 7

Contributions

Forgiveness is the giving,
and so the receiving, of life.

~ George MacDonald

In 2006, noted tycoon and philanthropist Warren Buffet stirred a small tornado whose aftershocks rocked the globe when he announced that he was giving away a fortune worth a whopping $40 billion. The news came as a shock because although Buffet is famous for his philanthropy, everyone thought he would donate his money to charity *after* his death. But to revise his timetable and give away a staggering fortune during his lifetime is unbelievable.

According to Buffet, a dominant portion of the gift will go to the Bill and Melinda Gates Foundation whose activities are focused on world health - fighting such diseases as malaria, HIV/AIDS, and tuberculosis - and on improving U.S. libraries and high schools. Bill Gates, of course, owns half of the planet along with Buffet. And his foundation, which he runs with his wife Melinda, has an asset worth of $30 billion.

No doubt about it, the enormity of the endowment is the biggest in history. In an interview with *Fortune Magazine*, Buffet said that he was honoring his late wife with the gift and he was giving part of it to Bill and Melinda because "I'm getting two people enormously successful at something, where I've had a chance to see what they've done, where I know they will keep doing it - where they've done it with their own money, so they're not living in some fantasy world - and where in general I agree with their reasoning. If I've found the right vehicle for my goal, there's no reason to wait."

Buffet believed as Andrew Carnegie did "that huge fortunes that low in large part from society should in large part be returned to society." And Buffet is not the only one doing it, even his children have set up foundations of their own in an effort to 'give back to society' and improve lives less fortunate than their own.

Giving away to charity can be viewed in two ways: as a tax deductible scheme or as a means to create and attract more wealth. You give back to the universe and the universe pays you back by giving you more than you expected.

Like Buffet and Gates, the Acquire Group of Companies basically follows the same rule. From day one, the company decided that it would give back. I set up a bank account and deposited 10% of our gross income into this account. At the end of the first twelve months, I gave away 20% of the balance and reinvested the rest. I look back at what I had set out to do and sometimes I had more money in our charity account than I did in our trading account. I do know though that the minute (at least that week) I gave away our first lot of monies, our business picked up and has not looked back.

From that bank account, I have now formalized it into a foundation called Your Gift Their Future Foundation, which works under the theme 'hands up not hand outs'. The foundation's aim is to accelerate growth through investments that will in turn be either distributed as financial donations, provide scholarships or similar support, or purchase assets that directly support the growth and self-empowerment of those in need.

To date, the foundation already has its several success stories, including:

- Gift of Money to the StepUp Foundation which aims to provide goal setting and personal skills to young teenagers.

- Gift of Time to the StepUp Foundation by volunteering time as a Team Coach to support one of the teen groups.

- Gift of Time to the Disabled Surf riders Association by providing volunteers to assist helping physically and mentally disabled people to enjoy riding on a surf board out in the waves.

- Gift of Money to Kiva which coordinates the provision of 'interest-free' micro-loans to people and organisations wanting to start up a small business that will support their family and local community with the intent of paying back the loan in a designated time period.

- Gift of Money to the SAGE Foundation which provides schools and training to teachers in India to provide better education to the children of India in the more disadvantaged areas.

I truly believe that the wealthy keep their money because of the fact that most of them give so much back. I believe it was John De Martini who asked the question about wealth accumulation: "Why would the universe give you more money if you do not know what to do or what you do with the money you have?"

Help us change the world!

Do you want to have more control over where you give your time, your resources or your money? Then join up as a member of the 'Your Gift Their Future Foundation' today. I am looking for motivated people who wish to make a difference. By coming together we can make a difference.

- Gift of time

- Gift of resources

- Gift of money

You donate your way. For more information go to: www. YourGiftTheirFuture.com

Go on!

You could be the person we have been waiting for ...

So now I know how to protect wealth, but how do I create it?

In reality that is another whole book in itself. However what we will share with you is a bit of information now on what you need to do to create wealth. In today's world there are only four ways to Create wealth and they are:

1. Business

2. Property

3. Shares

4. Internet

There are hundreds of books on the above topics and we could easily write a hundred more with everything we have leant about the above. However what we will share with you is some simple information that may help you decide which one is best for you. I love building businesses. I also love helping others build businesses as well. For shares and the internet we have other people who love those areas of creating wealth (yes other people) creating it for us.

There is no reason why you cannot partner up with someone if their skill set and passion for one area is bigger than your own. You can set up a joint venture (JV) or partnerships and look to stay in your low. We have also split the internet into a separate class. Yes, you will be building a business online; however, it is not your traditional type of business and needs to be addressed separately.

So let's get to it.

Business

I simply love building businesses and currently I am working on six, plus a charity. I have made great money in business and it is where I truly am in my low. I have built several successful businesses over my lifetime. Have I made mistakes? You bet - lots of them. Fail fast is a term I like because if you are going to fail, then fail fast and get on with it. Failure is the best way to learn and grow. You must be careful though that your failure steers your business and does not sink it. If you plan to fail chances are it will steer you into a better position. If you do not plan to fail, well you've seen the movie The Titanic.

The one big mistake I made was not selling them at the right time. One of my businesses was valued at $450k at its peak. I decided to keep it. Within 6 months the market changed and I am now lucky to sell it for less than $100k. Luckily I still get income from it without working it.

Today business is not just setting up a shop and hoping customers walk through the door. No, today's customers are far more savvy and educated than ever before. They want the best product at the best price and then some. You need to ensure you are offering them plenty of value. There are also so many options when choosing a business to get in to. You can set one up yourself from scratch. You can buy a ready-made one. You can buy a franchise with all the systems in place and you have the support of the franchisor. Here are some tips to get started in whichever field or type of business you choose.

1. Write down what you are good at. There may be things that you have not thought of that you could turn into a business. If you are going to set up a business from scratch, do something that you know and are good at.

2. Create a business plan. Now some people say a one page business plan is enough and some say you need a one hundred-plus page document. One that simply suits the business you are trying to set up will suffice.

3. Systemize it as quickly as possible. The faster you do this, the faster it becomes saleable and you can work less in the business. Use written, audio and visual when systemizing your business. This way you will appeal to all the senses.

4. Don't reinvent the wheel. There are so many places where you can get anything you need for your business. For example email us at info@acquiregroup.com.au and we will send out our Business startup CD. It has over 50 templates you will need to help set up your business from business plans to cash flow calculators, HR templates, contracts etc.

The most important part is to choose the right team around you. Here are some guidelines on how to do that.

Building a Team

With financial matters becoming increasingly complex - changing tax regulations, new investment vehicles being developed, new revisions on estate planning laws - it's hard for a single person to keep track and manage. That is why you should consider forming a financial advisory team. Aside from keeping you constantly updated on financial news, sound advice from your financial team can help you make informed decisions to achieve your financial goals.

Before you build your team however, you must have an understanding of the type of support you need. For example, if you're looking for an estate planning expert, then don't hire a real estate attorney. Or if you want a CPA to handle your annual tax return, don't get a small business accountant.

Also, keep in mind that someone else's financial planner may not be right for you. Your goal is to find a financial planner who will understand and accommodate your particular investment status and personality.

Select Your Team

Referrals remain the most effective way to identify potential team members. Talk to your family, friends, and colleagues. Consult with your lawyer about people he knows, look at professional associations that list members on their website, or conduct a phone or personal interview to gather information about individual backgrounds.

When building that financial team you should be confident that each team member you select:

- Is experienced and can be trusted,

- Can provide the services you need to achieve your goals,

- Will take time to provide you with options while explaining the associated pros and cons, and

- Can regularly communicate in person, over the phone, or via e-mail.

Who should be in your financial advisory team?

Start your team by hiring a registered financial professional, who will serve as the backbone of your team by making sure that you get the most current information that concerns your business. Financial professionals usually have training in five financial areas: budgeting and investing, insurance, estate planning, retirement planning and tax management. Thus, they are able to coordinate your financial moves and help you reach your goals.

Aside from a financial professional, your financial team should also include a mortgage broker, an accountant, an attorney/estate planner, and an insurance agent. When you finally build your team, it is extremely important that each member of your team maintain a solid working relationship together and separately.

Questions to ask while interviewing a financial planner

Keep in mind that a financial planner's job is to be your partner. So keep that in mind when choosing someone for the job. Financial planners will help you manage your money, which is a serious responsibility. Interview at least three people for the job before you commit to a specific individual.

Here are some key questions to ask during the interview:

- What is their professional background and how long have they been giving formal financial advice?

- What memberships do they hold in professional associations?

- Ask for referrals from existing clients or seek testimonials

- Who are they or their firm licensed through? If they are affiliated with a bank or a major financial services company, will it affect the advice they give you or the products you recommend?

- Ask for a financial plan. Do they understand your financial goals and risk tolerance?

- What is their fee structure? How do they charge for their services? Do they work for commissions or other financial benefits? How much will this advice cost you?

- Are there any financial products, providers, or super funds they don't recommend? Why?

- How do they keep up to date with financial news and legislative changes?

Choosing a financial planner

Finding a good financial planner with limited or no conflicts of interest is difficult. You need time and effort to seek out the right person. These 10 characteristics can serve as a checklist when you're looking to hire a financial planner.

1. *They charge an hourly or a flat fee.* Planners have four pay structures: flat fee, hourly fee, commissions on sold products, and percentage of assets managed. If you're looking to hire a planner, don't get into the last two compensation plans unless it suits your needs.

2. *They educate you.* Don't hire a planner who withholds information and doesn't take the time to teach you the basics. A good financial planner should want you to know as much as they know so that eventually you can manage your own finances and refer all of your friends to him/her.

3. *They are not a friend, co-worker, or family.* Don't bring emotional bonds into financial decisions. Avoid the drama, and the highs and lows that can potentially damage your relationship and yield disastrous financial results.

4. *They are patient with their advice.* A good financial planner does not call you with urgent hot stock picks. When it comes to investing, there should be no sense of urgency but careful planning.

5. *They are a certified financial professional.* A good financial planner has some sort of highly valued certification like a Certified Public Account (CPA), Certified Financial Planner (CFP), or a Chartered Financial Consultant (ChFC). Demand to see their credentials and then verify the credentials with the respective organisation.

6. *They are up front about their strategy.* A good financial planner should have no qualms in telling you exactly how they plan to invest your money. Why? Usually, a good financial planner has a relatively passive investment strategy that they believe in and stick to.

7. *They care about more than just your investments.* A sound financial strategy involves a whole lot more than just the types of asset classes you want to invest in. A good financial planner must also invest time in taking a holistic look at your spending habits, debt obligations, and life goals.

8. *They have a good reputation.* It takes more than a good referral to find a sound financial planner. They must also

be respected and have good reputations amongst their list of clientele.

9. *They have never been disciplined by the authorities.* Check with regulating authorities to make sure that your financial adviser does not have any black marks against them.

10. *They invoke genuine trust.* If you feel a certain stressed energy when around an adviser, trust your instincts and get out of there. Without trust, it's not going to be a good business relationship. Start from point one and go and find yourself another suitable financial planner.

What to expect from your financial planner

Whether you realise it or not, your relationship with your financial planner is going to be more closely intimate than your marriage, which means that expectations are higher as it involves money and the future of the rest of your family. What should you expect from your financial planner? Here's a list:

1. Assess financial information like tax returns, investments, retirement programs, your Will and insurance policies

2. Review net worth statements, cash flow and debt structure, and make sound recommendations

3. Identify financial areas where you may need help like retirement income or tax-saving suggestions

4. Help you decide on financial and investment goals by laying out several possible options

5. Provide a clearly-written financial plan which is specific to your situation, and discuss whether you're comfortable with it

6. Help you implement your financial plan, including referring you to specialists like lenders, lawyers or accountants when necessary

7. Periodically review your situation and financial plan, and suggest options to improve the plan when needed

8. Provide monthly or quarterly statement reports about the performance of your account, including worth, past transactions, and average returns

NEVER HIRE SOMEONE YOU CANNOT FIRE!

Mortgage broker

People often confuse mortgage brokers with lenders. A mortgage broker offers loan products, while a lender provides the actual loan money to the borrower. A mortgage broker essentially serves as a liaison between borrower and lender. A broker can work independently or within a firm.

Though a mortgage broker doesn't loan money, he works with borrowers by assisting them in finding appropriately matched mortgage loans. A mortgage broker shops for the best loan deal from lenders and matches the right lender with each individual client.

Since they work with many lenders, brokers are in a position to find loans suitable for borrowers with special needs, like credit problems. Brokers negotiate rates and terms with lenders as well as gather necessary documents, including credit reports, asset disclosures, employment verifications, property appraisals and asset disclosures. Once this is done, the mortgage broker submits the application to the lender, who then approves and disburses the loan.

In some cases, a mortgage broker also provides basic credit counseling to assist borrowers with credit issues. The mortgage broker's job starts before the loan process is completed. Once the borrower has obtained a mortgage, the broker's responsibility ends and all subsequent questions are asked of the lender.

Brokers earn commissions for bringing borrowers and lenders together. The commission is paid by the lender and not by the borrower. When the loan is closed, the mortgage broker then gets the commission.

Top 10 things to look for in a good mortgage broker

Because of the nature of their jobs, mortgage brokers don't really enjoy good reputations. Some have been involved in unethical, even illegal dealings, which don't really inspire confidence.

It doesn't mean, however, that you stop dealing with one altogether. What you shouldn't do is to start to limit your mortgage shopping to a single broker, and brokers don't expect you to. Nor should you stop at just a couple of brokers.

Here are ten things to look for in an ethical, reliable and dependable mortgage broker:

1. *They may charge a small processing fee.* Generally, your only out of pocket expense should be the cost of the application, which is paid directly to the appraisal company at the time of the appraisal. You could also ask them how much commission is paid by each lender. Professional brokers will provide this without hesitation. If your broker is unwilling to do so, proceed with caution. Some quality brokers, however, may charge a small processing fee normally around $497.

2. *They will explain terms and jargons that are unfamiliar to you.* A good broker shouldn't ask you to run to a real estate dictionary every time you have a conversation. They should explain what they mean. If they don't, it means they are using your lack of knowledge to confuse you.

3. *They will redo the numbers as many times as it takes for you to understand them.* Don't be embarrassed if you don't know anything about breakdown of payments, rates, terms, fees, loan amount, etc. Again, don't be embarrassed to show that you don't know. Instead, use this as a learning experience.

4. *They are always available.* A good broker must give you priority. It shouldn't take them a week to return your call or email.

5. *They under-promise and over-deliver.* There should not be any nasty surprises at the end of negotiations. From

the beginning, you should have been provided with a fair estimate of the loan process and if anything changes at the closing, you should benefit from it.

6. *They get your pre-qualifications done within an hour.* If you're in the process of being pre-qualified, your broker should be on top of things helping you look for prospective loan products. If they impede your progress then go back to square one and look for another candidate.

7. *They work with a good number of lenders.* You don't need a broker who's in the pocket of only one or two lenders. They don't serve your interest, but rather the interest of the lender. You need someone who looks out for your best interest and your situation.

8. They are intelligent and knowledgeable. A good broker may not have all the answers but they sure do have many of them. They are not only intelligent but listen when you speak.

9. They do not answer the question if they don't know the answer. Beware of a broker who promises you many things and changes their story thirty-five times. It's natural for changes to occur during a loan process but you need to find someone who can admit they don't know and find you the answer immediately.

10. They are personable. When dealing with someone with whom you're going to have a great deal of contact, there is no time for personality clashes. Your broker should make you feel comfortable at all times.

When to use a mortgage broker

You need a mortgage broker when you want the best deal for a loan. With their wide experience brokering a deal, a good mortgage broker can easily assist you to find what you want and what best suits your situation.

You're comparing prices and you need an expert opinion

You want a specific kind of loan but as rates and terms change daily, it is advisable that you take an entire week day before making all your calls. This may sound severe but then there's no other way to compare apples to apples.

You could start with one or two credit unions, then a few community banks. Next, try a few big national banks. Try the bank that has your checking account. They might offer you a deal. If you're refinancing, don't forget your current lender.

Next, call a few mortgage brokers that people you trust have recommended. Remember, it's not a breach of etiquette if you talk to more than one mortgage broker. You'll be making the largest financial decision of your life. The rule in hiring a mortgage broker is: if you have the time, why not check out what everybody else has?

You want the best rates and deals you can find

You're looking to land a good loan and you need the best rates and deals you can find. If your mortgage broker can find your perfect match, the next thing to ask is how precisely they will be paid. In general, brokers either make money directly from you via a fee of some sort or they get money from the lender. In some cases, it may be a combination of the two.

Brokers may tell you their fee comes from the bank, which is fine. But if the banks offer more money to brokers who push certain loans or terms at the cost of the borrower, then you'd best consult an accountant or a friend whose compensation does not depend on the answer.

Accountant

An accountant's job entails working to ensure that business firms and individuals keep good records and pay taxes properly and on time. Though the job description for some accounting positions may be simple, others are not quite as clear because of the number of duties it covers.

Accountants in general perform vital functions to businesses and individuals by offering a very wide array of business and accounting services, including public, management and government accounting, as well as internal auditing. There are four major fields of accounting with a separate job description:

1. Public Accountant

The job description of a public accountant can be summed up as 'typical' accounting work. It involves performing a broad range of accounting, auditing, tax, and consulting activities for corporate, government, nonprofit organisation, and individual clients.

Public accounting specialties are often chosen. For instance, a public accountant may choose to concentrate on advising companies about the tax advantages and disadvantages of certain business decisions and preparing individual income tax returns. Other public accountants may choose to specialise in areas such as compensation or employee health care benefits, accounting and data processing systems, and auditing financial statements. Public accounts are usually Certified Public Accountants (CPAs). They either work for their own businesses or for public accounting firms.

2. Management Accountant

A management accountant specialises in cost, managerial, industrial, corporate, or private accounts. They manage accountant records and analyse the financial information of the companies for which they work.

The management accountant's job includes budgeting, performance evaluation, cost management, and asset management. More often than not, they are a part of executive teams involved in strategic planning or the development of new products.

Their job is to analyse and interpret financial information that corporate executives need in order to make sound business decisions. They also prepare financial reports for stock holders, creditors, regulatory agencies and tax authorities.

3. Government accountant

A government accountant works in the public sector. They maintain and examine the records of government agencies and private businesses and individuals whose activities are subject to government regulation and/or taxation. Government account jobs are much more specialised as they are employed by Federal, State, or local governments, and work to guarantee that revenues are received and expenditures are made in accordance with laws and regulations.

4. Internal auditor accountant

An internal auditor's job is to verify the accuracy of an organisation's internal records, and check for mismanagement, waste or fraud. An increasingly important area of accounting, internal auditing, involves examining and evaluating a firm's financial and information systems, management procedures, and internal controls to ensure that records are accurate and controls are adequate to protect against fraud and waste.

Internal auditors also review company operations, evaluate their efficiency, effectiveness, and compliance with corporate policies and procedures, laws, and government regulations.

Why hiring an accountant is important

The services of a good accountant are invaluable to any business. First of all, an accountant can help you navigate the maze of tax laws as well as provide you the financial advice needed to manage and grow your business. Accountants keep you abreast of tax changes and tell you how a move could affect your taxes and/or your business's growth.

If you have not already hired an accountant for your business, it's about time you think of getting one.

Like most professions, accountants are a dime a dozen so how would you go about finding a good one?

1) Talk to your friends or business associates

Ask your friends who they use and how satisfied they are with the services provided by their accountant. If you can't get any good referrals, use the phone book and choose several accounting firms. When you call, ask the receptionist for the name(s) of accountants familiar with your type of business. Create a shortlist out of this information.

2) Select the best and discuss their services

Don't be embarrassed to ask your prospect about their education (whether or not they are a CPA), their experience with your industry, and their fees.

3) Prepare a set of questions you want to ask prospective accountants

The important thing to remember when shopping for an accountant is that besides their reputation and educational background, the ideal accountant is someone who is familiar with the special requirements of your business and/or your tax situation. For example:

- If your business is Internet related then you'll want an accountant who is familiar with the language of e-commerce.

- If your business involves periods of work in the U.S., you need an accountant who knows their way around the IRS and has experience completing U.S. tax forms.

- If you're into exporting, ask how the accountant might help you develop an export strategy.

Below are some sample questions you can ask a prospective accountant during an interview:

- What can you do to help my business grow? Ask for an outline in writing.

- If my business goes through a growth period, how can I get additional financing so that I don't go bust? Ask for specifics like which lenders will loan you money and how long will it take to get the money.

- Are you a tax planner or just a tax preparer? You may meet with your accountant once a year for strategic and tax planning so you will need more than a tax preparer to brainstorm with.

- What benchmarks will you help me set for my business so I can track my projects? An accountant who specialises in small business finances would be able to help you set month-by-month goals to chart your progress.

- How tech savvy is the accountant? Are you still using hard copies or simply transferring everything electronically? What kind of software will you have to buy? Remember, your CPA charges an hourly fee so electronic transfers can cut down the time your CPA uses to go through your financials.

- What overall services can the accountant provide besides business advice? As the financial halfback of your business, can he or she find outside experts to help meet your goals, like attorneys, insurance agents, real estate agents, etc.?

4. Choose someone with broad experience

Your business accountant should be more than just a tax preparer. They should also be a strategic and tax planner who will help you take advantage of tax laws during the business year.

It is important that you find the right people to work with and build your perfect team. Growing and protecting your wealth is more than knowing the right decision to make but also in having the right people you trust by your side when you make that crucial decision. Look at it this way, to win a war you need good and trustworthy generals to carry out your campaign. Without them, you cannot expect to run, let alone win a war on your own.

Property

Property is the golden child in Australia. We love property, and why not? Despite changes to the Government, wars, interest rate changes, and migration, property has doubled every 7 to 10 years for the last 120 years!

Other factors to consider are the number of people owning their own home is decreasing while the number of people who are renting these days is increasing. The demand for property has increased, while the supply has decreased. Australia's population grew over 439,000 in 2009 alone, so with all these factors to consider how do you go about making money in property?

First, decide which strategy you are going to use. The main strategies are:

- Discount

- Reno

- Strata

- Subdivide

- Off the plan

- Development.

If I am hopeless with tools, would a renovation be a good strategy for me? Well, if I paid someone to do the work for me, then yes. If I was to do it on my own, then no way.

They say you should fall in love with the deal NOT the property. I have seen over the years that 9 times out of 10 someone loses money on a deal because they got emotional about the property. Emotions and investing are a dangerous mix and should not cross at any cost.

Shares and the internet we will leave for another time. But remember, whichever way you decide to go, whether it is businesses, property, shares or the internet - please ensure you get an **expert team** and NOT a team of experts!

Conclusion

I hope the information has helped you realize that protecting your wealth is an essential part of the wealth creation plan. No matter what you are doing or wanting to achieve, the start of any journey starts with the first step. Take action NOW - not next week, not next month, but TODAY. Do it today.

We have created this book so that you have the tools you need to protect your wealth. You will save genuine money by using ALL the bonuses within this book, including access to some of the best experts in this country in their fields - accounting, finance, financial planning and business coaching. No other book allows you to do this. I encourage you right now to rip out the page titled 'I promise'. Sign it and put it on your wall. Without the commitment to change, you never will. Go to our website and become a member. Sign up for my monthly newsletter. Talk to me about what you want to achieve and I will help you get there.

Winners...

... **TAKE CHANCES**. Like everyone else they fear failing, but they refuse to let fear control them.

... **DON'T GIVE UP.** When life gets rough they hang in until the going gets better.

... **ARE FLEXIBLE.** They realise there is more than one way and are willing to try others.

... **KNOW THEY ARE NOT PERFECT**. They respect their weaknesses while making the most of their strengths.

... **FALL, BUT THEY DON'T STAY DOWN.** They stubbornly refuse to let a fall keep them from climbing.

... **DON'T BLAME FATE** for their failures nor their luck for their success.

... **ACCEPT RESPONSIBILTY** for their lives.

... **ARE POSITIVE THINKERS** who see good in all things. From the ordinary, they make the extraordinary.

... **BELIEVE IN THE PATH** they have chosen even when it is hard, even when others can't see where they are going.

... **ARE PATIENT.** They know a goal is only as worthy as the effort that's required to achieve it.

Nancye Sims

I promise ...

I .... promise myself that I will do whatever it takes to create the life I want and deserve. I know with the right team and the right attitude I will succeed in whatever I put my mind to. I will look back someday and thank myself for this commitment.

Regards,

X ....

Glossary of terms for finance

Basic Home Loan:	Don't need 'bells and whistles'; a basic loan could be the answer. In most cases the features that are offered with loans come at a cost. If you don't need them why pay for them?
Bridging Loan:	Loans that are provided to enable you to buy your next home before waiting for the sale of the existing home. In some cases the interest can be added to the new loan.
Construction Loan:	A loan that increases as the home is built. The lender usually checks the stage of completion before releasing funds to the builder. You only pay interest on the actual amount outstanding and in some cases payments can be deferred until the home is completed.
Default:	The failure to fulfill an obligation under the loan contract or Mortgage; such as not making loan repayments.
Equity:	The difference between the value of your home and the amount of the loan that is outstanding.

Fixed Rate Loan: A loan where the interest rate is fixed for an agreed time, usually one to five years. When the loan is approved the lender will provide an 'indicative rate'.

This is because the lender needs to commit to its own source of funds at the market rate on the day you need the money to settle. These rates can vary much more frequently than the variable rates that are quoted.

These loans are attractive in the case where the applicant wants to ix their commitments for a term, however can be penalised if it becomes necessary to break the contract.

During the course of the agreed term you may be paying a higher or lower rate than the variable rate.

Home Equity Loan: As the value of your home increases and the repayments reduce the loan, the equity will increase. Lenders can 'release' this amount in the form of an Equity Loan to be used for almost any purpose.

Home Improvement Loan: Additions to the home usually increase its value so lenders provide these loans to assist with the renovations.

Interest Offset: An account where any funds deposited effectively reduce the loan balance on which the interest is calculated. You still have full access to your money when needed. A great way to reduce the interest and term of your loan.

Investment Loan: A loan used to purchase an investment property.

Sometimes the equity in the home property is used instead of a deposit   o n the investment property loan.

Line of Credit: Effectively an overdraft account. Used well it can save interest but used badly can create problems. A full knowledge of these is required as well assa as good financial management.

Low Doc Loans: Loans that do not require the presentation of as much documentary evidence. Primarily for self-employed people.

Loan Contract: A document signed by the borrower and lender that sets out the details of the Loan. It should include all fees and the interest rate.

LVR:	Loan to Valuation Ratio. Lenders prefer to lend at 80%, but more and more loans are being written at higher LVRs of up to 95% as values increase and ability to accumulate deposits becomes more difficult.
No Deposit Home Loan:	Loans for 100% of the purchase price.
	Usually another source of security is provided.
No Doc Loans:	Loans with no supporting documentation. The lenders provide the funds purely based on the value of the property. Typically a lower LVR is available and the interest rate is higher.
Pre-Approval Loans:	It is possible to apply and obtain approval for a loan without a particular property in mind. It can be very useful when negotiating a purchase price with the vendor to let them know that you have a loan pre-approved. The approval will be subject to a number of conditions so make sure that you do not sign an unconditional contract to purchase the property until you have unconditional approval from the lender.
Professional Packages:	Loans with special features that appeal to people on a higher income.

Redraw Facility: A loan feature that allows you to deposit increased repayments when the   money is available and then draw it out when required. Check the details as sometimes there is a fee and limits on amounts.

Second Home Loan: A loan to purchase a second or holiday home.

Settlement: The event that involves the vendor receiving their money for the sale to the purchaser and in exchange hands over the title of ownership. Usually carried out by solicitors or land brokers appointed by each party to protect their interests throughout the transaction.

Split Rate Home Loan: Part of the loan is at a fixed rate and part at the variable rate. Brings the benefits of variable and fixed interest rates into a single home loan.

Standard Variable Rate Home Loan: A standard home loan offers a mix of features, flexibility, interest rates and fees.

Variable Interest Rate: The interest rate charged on the loan is subject to market fluctuations and can rise or fall from time to time. In a rising market you may be called on to increase repayments to meet the higher cost in a falling market your loan will reduce more quickly.

Vendor: The people selling the house.

www.ingramcontent.com/pod-product-compliance
Lightning Source LLC
Chambersburg PA
CBHW071556200326
41519CB00021BB/6776